# This planner belongs to:

_______________

© Copyright Shy Panda Notebooks. All rights reserved.

# Twenty-one

## January

| S | M | T | W | T | F | S |
|---|---|---|---|---|---|---|
|   |   |   |   |   | 1 | 2 |
| 3 | 4 | 5 | 6 | 7 | 8 | 9 |
| 10 | 11 | 12 | 13 | 14 | 15 | 16 |
| 17 | 18 | 19 | 20 | 21 | 22 | 23 |
| 24 | 25 | 26 | 27 | 28 | 29 | 30 |
| 31 |   |   |   |   |   |   |

## February

| S | M | T | W | T | F | S |
|---|---|---|---|---|---|---|
|   | 1 | 2 | 3 | 4 | 5 | 6 |
| 7 | 8 | 9 | 10 | 11 | 12 | 13 |
| 14 | 15 | 16 | 17 | 18 | 19 | 20 |
| 21 | 22 | 23 | 24 | 25 | 26 | 27 |
| 28 |   |   |   |   |   |   |

## March

| S | M | T | W | T | F | S |
|---|---|---|---|---|---|---|
|   | 1 | 2 | 3 | 4 | 5 | 6 |
| 7 | 8 | 9 | 10 | 11 | 12 | 13 |
| 14 | 15 | 16 | 17 | 18 | 19 | 20 |
| 21 | 22 | 23 | 24 | 25 | 26 | 27 |
| 28 | 29 | 30 | 31 |   |   |   |

## April

| S | M | T | W | T | F | S |
|---|---|---|---|---|---|---|
|   |   |   |   | 1 | 2 | 3 |
| 4 | 5 | 6 | 7 | 8 | 9 | 10 |
| 11 | 12 | 13 | 14 | 15 | 16 | 17 |
| 18 | 19 | 20 | 21 | 22 | 23 | 24 |
| 25 | 26 | 27 | 28 | 29 | 30 |   |

## May

| S | M | T | W | T | F | S |
|---|---|---|---|---|---|---|
|   |   |   |   |   |   | 1 |
| 2 | 3 | 4 | 5 | 6 | 7 | 8 |
| 9 | 10 | 11 | 12 | 13 | 14 | 15 |
| 16 | 17 | 18 | 19 | 20 | 21 | 22 |
| 23 | 24 | 25 | 26 | 27 | 28 | 29 |
| 30 | 31 |   |   |   |   |   |

## June

| S | M | T | W | T | F | S |
|---|---|---|---|---|---|---|
|   |   | 1 | 2 | 3 | 4 | 5 |
| 6 | 7 | 8 | 9 | 10 | 11 | 12 |
| 13 | 14 | 15 | 16 | 17 | 18 | 19 |
| 20 | 21 | 22 | 23 | 24 | 25 | 26 |
| 27 | 28 | 29 | 30 |   |   |   |

## July

| S | M | T | W | T | F | S |
|---|---|---|---|---|---|---|
|   |   |   |   | 1 | 2 | 3 |
| 4 | 5 | 6 | 7 | 8 | 9 | 10 |
| 11 | 12 | 13 | 14 | 15 | 16 | 17 |
| 18 | 19 | 20 | 21 | 22 | 23 | 24 |
| 25 | 26 | 27 | 28 | 29 | 30 | 31 |

## August

| S | M | T | W | T | F | S |
|---|---|---|---|---|---|---|
| 1 | 2 | 3 | 4 | 5 | 6 | 7 |
| 8 | 9 | 10 | 11 | 12 | 13 | 14 |
| 15 | 16 | 17 | 18 | 19 | 20 | 21 |
| 22 | 23 | 24 | 25 | 26 | 27 | 28 |
| 29 | 30 | 31 |   |   |   |   |

## September

| S | M | T | W | T | F | S |
|---|---|---|---|---|---|---|
|   |   |   | 1 | 2 | 3 | 4 |
| 5 | 6 | 7 | 8 | 9 | 10 | 11 |
| 12 | 13 | 14 | 15 | 16 | 17 | 18 |
| 19 | 20 | 21 | 22 | 23 | 24 | 25 |
| 26 | 27 | 28 | 29 | 30 |   |   |

## October

| S | M | T | W | T | F | S |
|---|---|---|---|---|---|---|
|   |   |   |   |   | 1 | 2 |
| 3 | 4 | 5 | 6 | 7 | 8 | 9 |
| 10 | 11 | 12 | 13 | 14 | 15 | 16 |
| 17 | 18 | 19 | 20 | 21 | 22 | 23 |
| 24 | 25 | 26 | 27 | 28 | 29 | 30 |
| 31 |   |   |   |   |   |   |

## November

| S | M | T | W | T | F | S |
|---|---|---|---|---|---|---|
|   | 1 | 2 | 3 | 4 | 5 | 6 |
| 7 | 8 | 9 | 10 | 11 | 12 | 13 |
| 14 | 15 | 16 | 17 | 18 | 19 | 20 |
| 21 | 22 | 23 | 24 | 25 | 26 | 27 |
| 28 | 29 | 30 |   |   |   |   |

## December

| S | M | T | W | T | F | S |
|---|---|---|---|---|---|---|
|   |   |   | 1 | 2 | 3 | 4 |
| 5 | 6 | 7 | 8 | 9 | 10 | 11 |
| 12 | 13 | 14 | 15 | 16 | 17 | 18 |
| 19 | 20 | 21 | 22 | 23 | 24 | 25 |
| 26 | 27 | 28 | 29 | 30 | 31 |   |

# Year in Pixels

| | J | F | M | A | M | J | J | A | S | O | N | D |
|---|---|---|---|---|---|---|---|---|---|---|---|---|
| 1. | | | | | | | | | | | | |
| 2. | | | | | | | | | | | | |
| 3. | | | | | | | | | | | | |
| 4. | | | | | | | | | | | | |
| 5. | | | | | | | | | | | | |
| 6. | | | | | | | | | | | | |
| 7. | | | | | | | | | | | | |
| 8. | | | | | | | | | | | | |
| 9. | | | | | | | | | | | | |
| 10. | | | | | | | | | | | | |
| 11. | | | | | | | | | | | | |
| 12. | | | | | | | | | | | | |
| 13. | | | | | | | | | | | | |
| 14. | | | | | | | | | | | | |
| 15. | | | | | | | | | | | | |
| 16. | | | | | | | | | | | | |
| 17. | | | | | | | | | | | | |
| 18. | | | | | | | | | | | | |
| 19. | | | | | | | | | | | | |
| 20. | | | | | | | | | | | | |
| 21. | | | | | | | | | | | | |
| 22. | | | | | | | | | | | | |
| 23. | | | | | | | | | | | | |
| 24. | | | | | | | | | | | | |
| 25. | | | | | | | | | | | | |
| 26. | | | | | | | | | | | | |
| 27. | | | | | | | | | | | | |
| 28. | | | | | | | | | | | | |
| 29. | | | | | | | | | | | | |
| 30. | | | | | | | | | | | | |
| 31. | | | | | | | | | | | | |

## Color Codes

## Notes

# January 2021

| SUNDAY | MONDAY | TUESDAY | WEDNESDAY |
|---|---|---|---|
|  |  |  |  |
| 3 | 4 | 5 | 6 |
| 10 | 11 | 12 | 13 |
| 17 | 18 | 19 | 20 |
| 24 | 25 | 26 | 27 |

# January 2021

| THURSDAY | FRIDAY | SATURDAY | NOTES |
|---|---|---|---|
|  | 1 | 2 | ○ |
|  |  |  | ○ |
|  |  |  | ○ |
|  |  |  | ○ |
|  |  |  | ○ |
| 7 | 8 | 9 | ○ |
|  |  |  | ○ |
|  |  |  | ○ |
|  |  |  | ○ |
| 14 | 15 | 16 | ○ |
|  |  |  | ○ |
|  |  |  | ○ |
|  |  |  | ○ |
|  |  |  | ○ |
| 21 | 22 | 23 | ○ |
|  |  |  | ○ |
|  |  |  | ○ |
|  |  |  | ○ |
|  |  |  | ○ |
| 28 | 29 | 30 | 31 |

# February 2021

| SUNDAY | MONDAY | TUESDAY | WEDNESDAY |
|---|---|---|---|
|  | 1 | 2 | 3 |
| 7 | 8 | 9 | 10 |
| 14 | 15 | 16 | 17 |
| 21 | 22 | 23 | 24 |
| 28 |  |  |  |

# February 2021

| THURSDAY | FRIDAY | SATURDAY | NOTES |
|---|---|---|---|
| 4 | 5 | 6 | ○ |
| | | | ○ |
| | | | ○ |
| | | | ○ |
| | | | ○ |
| 11 | 12 | 13 | ○ |
| | | | ○ |
| | | | ○ |
| | | | ○ |
| 18 | 19 | 20 | ○ |
| | | | ○ |
| | | | ○ |
| | | | ○ |
| | | | ○ |
| 25 | 26 | 27 | ○ |
| | | | ○ |
| | | | ○ |
| | | | ○ |
| | | | ○ |
| | | | NOTES |

# March 2021

| SUNDAY | MONDAY | TUESDAY | WEDNESDAY |
|---|---|---|---|
|  | 1 | 2 | 3 |
| 7 | 8 | 9 | 10 |
| 14 | 15 | 16 | 17 |
| 21 | 22 | 23 | 24 |
| 28 | 29 | 30 | 31 |

# March 2021

| THURSDAY | FRIDAY | SATURDAY | NOTES |
|---|---|---|---|
| 4 | 5 | 6 | ○ |
| | | | ○ |
| | | | ○ |
| | | | ○ |
| | | | ○ |
| 11 | 12 | 13 | ○ |
| | | | ○ |
| | | | ○ |
| | | | ○ |
| 18 | 19 | 20 | ○ |
| | | | ○ |
| | | | ○ |
| | | | ○ |
| | | | ○ |
| 25 | 26 | 27 | ○ |
| | | | ○ |
| | | | ○ |
| | | | ○ |
| | | | ○ |
| | | | NOTES |

# April 2021

| SUNDAY | MONDAY | TUESDAY | WEDNESDAY |
| --- | --- | --- | --- |
|  |  |  |  |
| 4 | 5 | 6 | 7 |
| 11 | 12 | 13 | 14 |
| 18 | 19 | 20 | 21 |
| 25 | 26 | 27 | 28 |

| THURSDAY | FRIDAY | SATURDAY | NOTES |
|---|---|---|---|
| 1 | 2 | 3 | ○ |
|  |  |  | ○ |
|  |  |  | ○ |
|  |  |  | ○ |
|  |  |  | ○ |
| 8 | 9 | 10 | ○ |
|  |  |  | ○ |
|  |  |  | ○ |
|  |  |  | ○ |
| 15 | 16 | 17 | ○ |
|  |  |  | ○ |
|  |  |  | ○ |
|  |  |  | ○ |
|  |  |  | ○ |
| 22 | 23 | 24 | ○ |
|  |  |  | ○ |
|  |  |  | ○ |
|  |  |  | ○ |
|  |  |  | ○ |
| 29 | 30 | 1 | NOTES |

# May *2021*

| SUNDAY | MONDAY | TUESDAY | WEDNESDAY |
|---|---|---|---|
| 2 | 3 | 4 | 5 |
| 9 | 10 | 11 | 12 |
| 16 | 17 | 18 | 19 |
| 23 | 24 | 25 | 26 |
| 30 | 31 | | |

# May 2021

| THURSDAY | FRIDAY | SATURDAY | NOTES |
|---|---|---|---|
| 6 | 7 | 8 | ○ |
| | | | ○ |
| | | | ○ |
| | | | ○ |
| | | | ○ |
| 13 | 14 | 15 | ○ |
| | | | ○ |
| | | | ○ |
| | | | ○ |
| 20 | 21 | 22 | ○ |
| | | | ○ |
| | | | ○ |
| | | | ○ |
| | | | ○ |
| 27 | 28 | 29 | ○ |
| | | | ○ |
| | | | ○ |
| | | | ○ |
| | | | ○ |
| | | | NOTES |

# June 2021

| SUNDAY | MONDAY | TUESDAY | WEDNESDAY |
|---|---|---|---|
|  |  | 1 | 2 |
| 6 | 7 | 8 | 9 |
| 13 | 14 | 15 | 16 |
| 20 | 21 | 22 | 23 |
| 27 | 28 | 29 | 30 |

# June



| THURSDAY | FRIDAY | SATURDAY | NOTES |
|---|---|---|---|
| 3 | 4 | 5 | ○ |
|  |  |  | ○ |
|  |  |  | ○ |
|  |  |  | ○ |
|  |  |  | ○ |
| 10 | 11 | 12 | ○ |
|  |  |  | ○ |
|  |  |  | ○ |
|  |  |  | ○ |
|  |  |  | ○ |
| 17 | 18 | 19 | ○ |
|  |  |  | ○ |
|  |  |  | ○ |
|  |  |  | ○ |
|  |  |  | ○ |
| 24 | 25 | 26 | ○ |
|  |  |  | ○ |
|  |  |  | ○ |
|  |  |  | ○ |
|  |  |  | ○ |
|  |  |  | NOTES |

# July 2021

| SUNDAY | MONDAY | TUESDAY | WEDNESDAY |
|---|---|---|---|
|  |  |  |  |
| 4 | 5 | 6 | 7 |
| 11 | 12 | 13 | 14 |
| 18 | 19 | 20 | 21 |
| 25 | 26 | 27 | 28 |

# July 2021

| THURSDAY | FRIDAY | SATURDAY | NOTES |
|---|---|---|---|
| 1 | 2 | 3 | ○ |
| | | | ○ |
| | | | ○ |
| | | | ○ |
| | | | ○ |
| 8 | 9 | 10 | ○ |
| | | | ○ |
| | | | ○ |
| | | | ○ |
| | | | ○ |
| 15 | 16 | 17 | ○ |
| | | | ○ |
| | | | ○ |
| | | | ○ |
| | | | ○ |
| 22 | 23 | 24 | ○ |
| | | | ○ |
| | | | ○ |
| | | | ○ |
| | | | ○ |
| 29 | 30 | 31 | NOTES |

# August 2021

| SUNDAY | MONDAY | TUESDAY | WEDNESDAY |
|---|---|---|---|
| 1 | 2 | 3 | 4 |
| 8 | 9 | 10 | 11 |
| 15 | 16 | 17 | 18 |
| 22 | 23 | 24 | 25 |
| 29 | 30 | 31 | |

# August 2021

| THURSDAY | FRIDAY | SATURDAY | NOTES |
|---|---|---|---|
| 5 | 6 | 7 | ○ |
|  |  |  | ○ |
|  |  |  | ○ |
|  |  |  | ○ |
|  |  |  | ○ |
| 12 | 13 | 14 | ○ |
|  |  |  | ○ |
|  |  |  | ○ |
|  |  |  | ○ |
|  |  |  | ○ |
| 19 | 20 | 21 | ○ |
|  |  |  | ○ |
|  |  |  | ○ |
|  |  |  | ○ |
|  |  |  | ○ |
| 26 | 27 | 28 | NOTES |
|  |  |  |  |

# September 2021

| SUNDAY | MONDAY | TUESDAY | WEDNESDAY |
|---|---|---|---|
|  |  |  | 1 |
| 5 | 6 | 7 | 8 |
| 12 | 13 | 14 | 15 |
| 19 | 20 | 21 | 22 |
| 26 | 27 | 28 | 29 |

# September 2021

| THURSDAY | FRIDAY | SATURDAY | NOTES |
|---|---|---|---|
| 2 | 3 | 4 | ○ |
| | | | ○ |
| | | | ○ |
| | | | ○ |
| | | | ○ |
| 9 | 10 | 11 | ○ |
| | | | ○ |
| | | | ○ |
| | | | ○ |
| 16 | 17 | 18 | ○ |
| | | | ○ |
| | | | ○ |
| | | | ○ |
| | | | ○ |
| 23 | 24 | 25 | ○ |
| | | | ○ |
| | | | ○ |
| | | | ○ |
| | | | ○ |
| 30 | | | NOTES |

# October 2021

| SUNDAY | MONDAY | TUESDAY | WEDNESDAY |
| --- | --- | --- | --- |
|  |  |  |  |
| 3 | 4 | 5 | 6 |
| 10 | 11 | 12 | 13 |
| 17 | 18 | 19 | 20 |
| 24 | 25 | 26 | 27 |

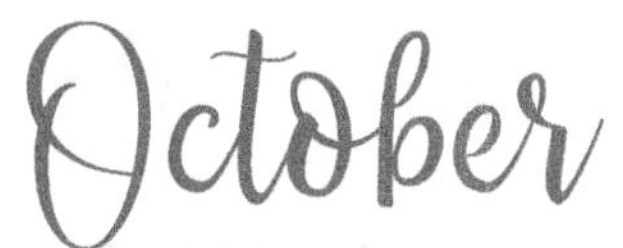

# October 2021

| THURSDAY | FRIDAY | SATURDAY | NOTES |
|---|---|---|---|
|  | 1 | 2 | ○ |
|  |  |  | ○ |
|  |  |  | ○ |
|  |  |  | ○ |
|  |  |  | ○ |
| 7 | 8 | 9 | ○ |
|  |  |  | ○ |
|  |  |  | ○ |
|  |  |  | ○ |
| 14 | 15 | 16 | ○ |
|  |  |  | ○ |
|  |  |  | ○ |
|  |  |  | ○ |
|  |  |  | ○ |
| 21 | 22 | 23 | ○ |
|  |  |  | ○ |
|  |  |  | ○ |
|  |  |  | ○ |
|  |  |  | ○ |
| 28 | 29 | 30 | NOTES |
|  |  | 31 SUNDAY |  |

# November 2021

| SUNDAY | MONDAY | TUESDAY | WEDNESDAY |
|---|---|---|---|
|  | 1 | 2 | 3 |
| 7 | 8 | 9 | 10 |
| 14 | 15 | 16 | 17 |
| 21 | 22 | 23 | 24 |
| 28 | 29 | 30 |  |

| THURSDAY | FRIDAY | SATURDAY | NOTES |
|---|---|---|---|
| 4 | 5 | 6 | ○ |
| | | | ○ |
| | | | ○ |
| | | | ○ |
| | | | ○ |
| 11 | 12 | 13 | ○ |
| | | | ○ |
| | | | ○ |
| | | | ○ |
| 18 | 19 | 20 | ○ |
| | | | ○ |
| | | | ○ |
| | | | ○ |
| | | | ○ |
| 25 | 26 | 27 | ○ |
| | | | ○ |
| | | | ○ |
| | | | ○ |
| | | | ○ |
| | | | NOTES |

# December 2021

| SUNDAY | MONDAY | TUESDAY | WEDNESDAY |
|---|---|---|---|
|  |  |  | 1 |
| 5 | 6 | 7 | 8 |
| 12 | 13 | 14 | 15 |
| 19 | 20 | 21 | 22 |
| 26 | 27 | 28 | 29 |

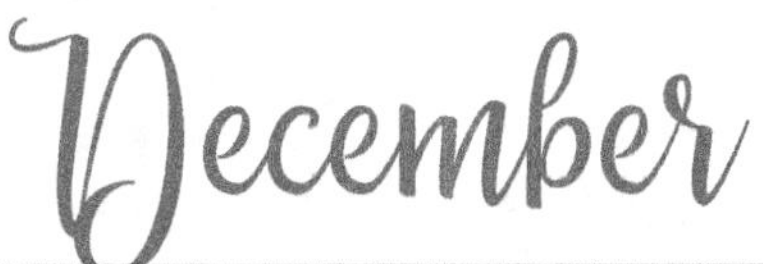

# December 2021

| THURSDAY | FRIDAY | SATURDAY | NOTES |
|---|---|---|---|
| 2 | 3 | 4 | ○ |
|  |  |  | ○ |
|  |  |  | ○ |
|  |  |  | ○ |
|  |  |  | ○ |
| 9 | 10 | 11 | ○ |
|  |  |  | ○ |
|  |  |  | ○ |
|  |  |  | ○ |
| 16 | 17 | 18 | ○ |
|  |  |  | ○ |
|  |  |  | ○ |
|  |  |  | ○ |
|  |  |  | ○ |
| 23 | 24 | 25 | ○ |
|  |  |  | ○ |
|  |  |  | ○ |
|  |  |  | ○ |
|  |  |  | ○ |
| 30 | 31 |  | NOTES |

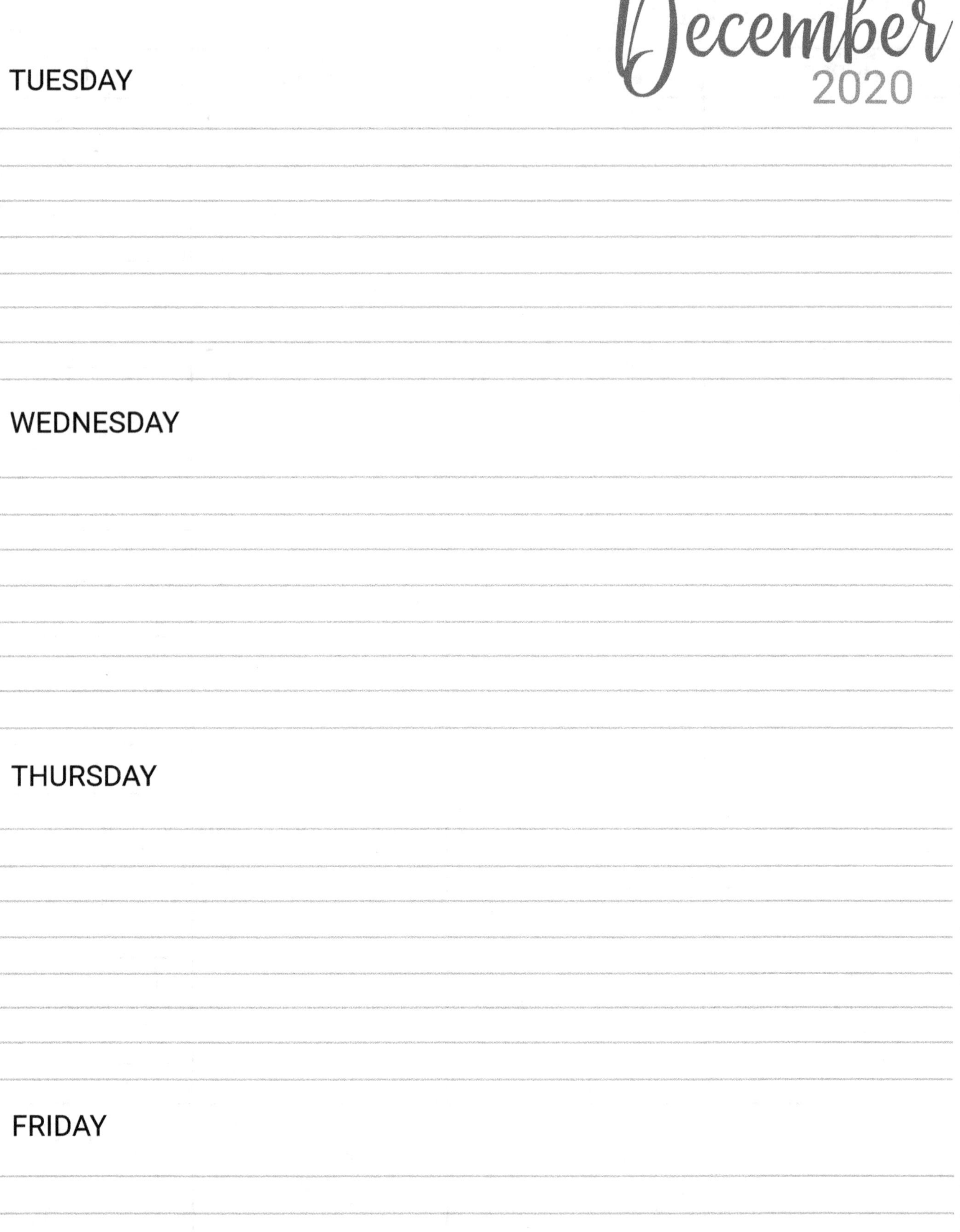


December
2020

01 TUESDAY

02 WEDNESDAY

03 THURSDAY

04 FRIDAY

# December
## 2020

**05** SATURDAY

**06** SUNDAY

**07** MONDAY

**08** TUESDAY

**09** WEDNESDAY

**10** THURSDAY

**11** FRIDAY

**12** SATURDAY

**13** SUNDAY

**14** MONDAY

**15** TUESDAY

**16** WEDNESDAY

## 17 THURSDAY

## 18 FRIDAY

## 19 SATURDAY

## 20 SUNDAY

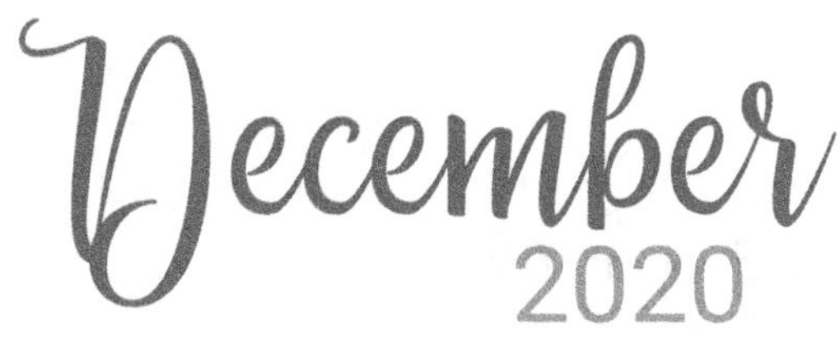



**21** MONDAY

**22** TUESDAY

**23** WEDNESDAY

**24** THURSDAY

**25** FRIDAY

○
○
○
○
○
○
○
○

**26** SATURDAY

○
○
○
○
○
○
○
○

**27** SUNDAY

○
○
○
○
○
○
○
○

**28** MONDAY

○
○
○
○
○

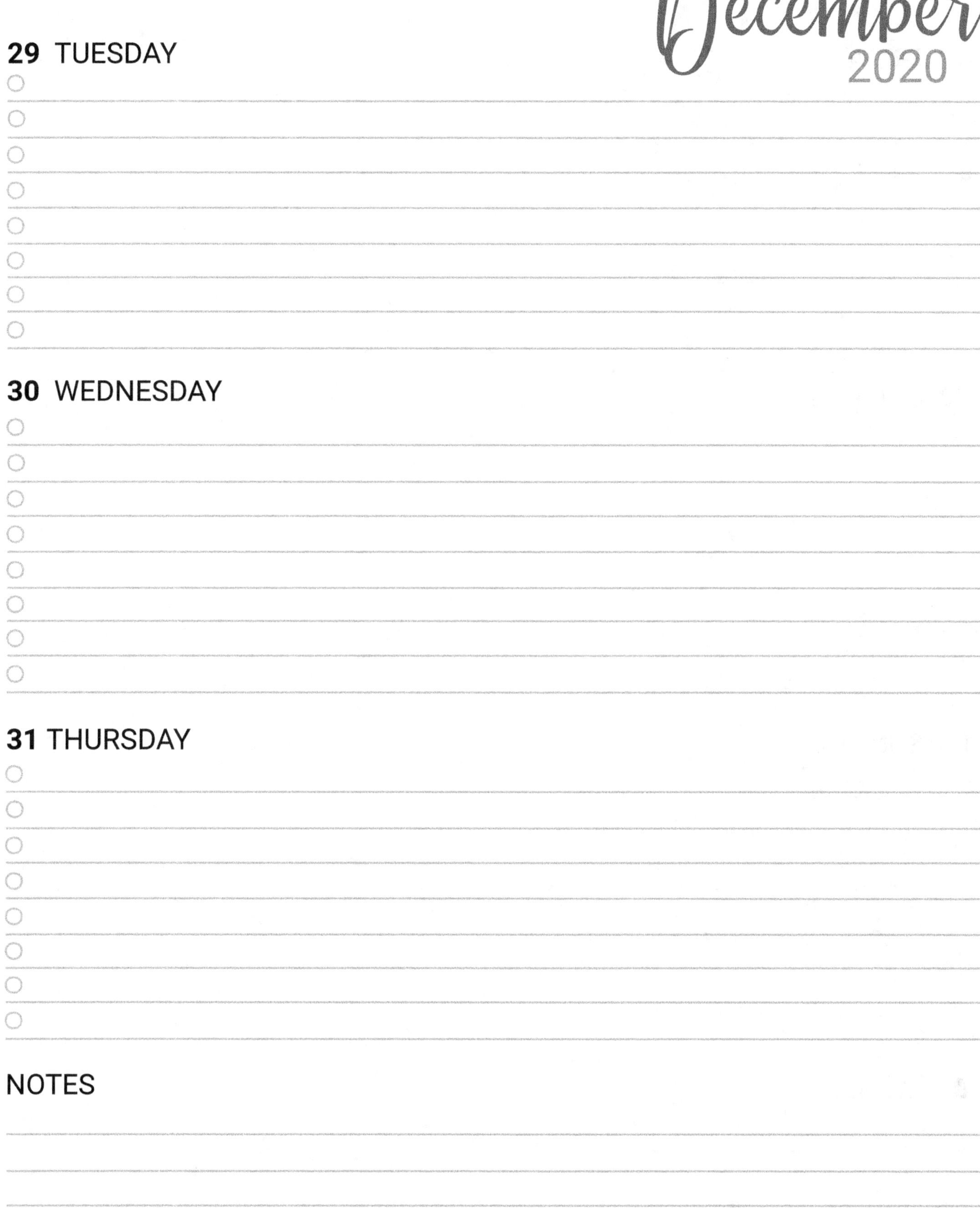



**29** TUESDAY

**30** WEDNESDAY

**31** THURSDAY

NOTES

**01** FRIDAY

○
○
○
○
○
○
○
○

**02** SATURDAY

○
○
○
○
○
○
○
○

**03** SUNDAY

○
○
○
○
○
○
○
○

**04** MONDAY

○
○
○
○
○

# January
## 2021

**05** TUESDAY

**06** WEDNESDAY

**07** THURSDAY

**08** FRIDAY

**09** SATURDAY

**10** SUNDAY

**11** MONDAY

**12** TUESDAY

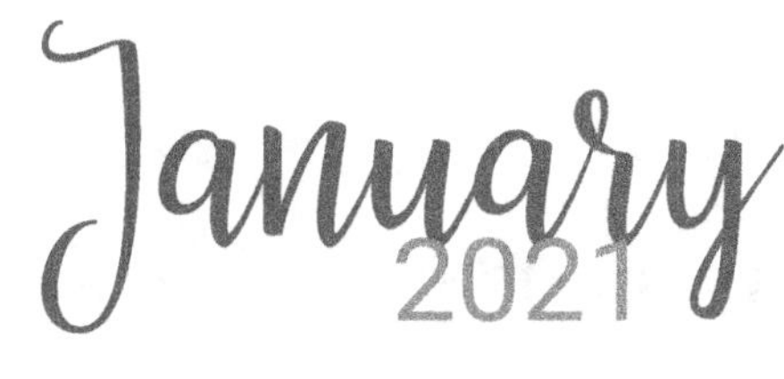


**13** WEDNESDAY

**14** THURSDAY

**15** FRIDAY

**16** SATURDAY

**17** SUNDAY

**18** MONDAY

**19** TUESDAY

**20** WEDNESDAY

# January 2021

## 21 THURSDAY

## 22 FRIDAY

## 23 SATURDAY

## 24 SUNDAY

**25** MONDAY

**26** TUESDAY

**27** WEDNESDAY

**28** THURSDAY

# January
## 2021

**29** FRIDAY

- ○
- ○
- ○
- ○
- ○
- ○
- ○
- ○

**30** SATURDAY

- ○
- ○
- ○
- ○
- ○
- ○
- ○
- ○

**31** SUNDAY

- ○
- ○
- ○
- ○
- ○
- ○
- ○
- ○

NOTES

**01** MONDAY

**02** TUESDAY

**03** WEDNESDAY

**04** THURSDAY

**05** FRIDAY

**06** SATURDAY

**07** SUNDAY

**08** MONDAY

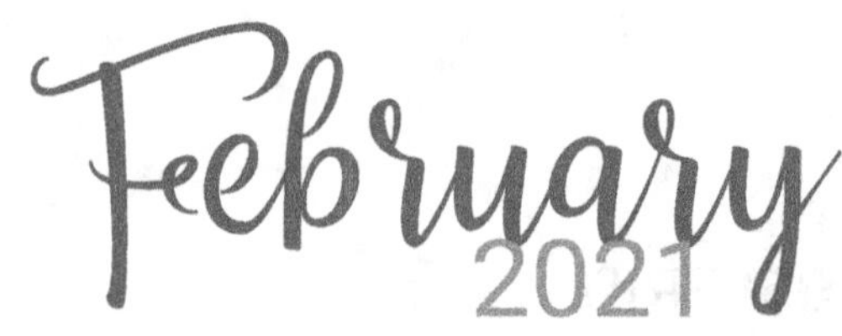


**09** TUESDAY

**10** WEDNESDAY

**11** THURSDAY

**12** FRIDAY

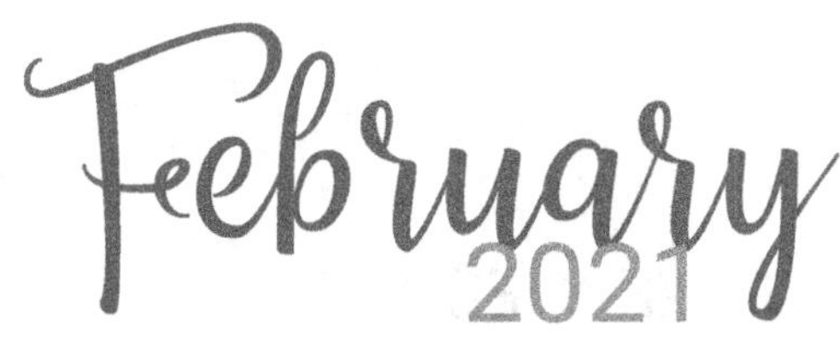



**13** SATURDAY

**14** SUNDAY

**15** MONDAY

**16** TUESDAY

**17** WEDNESDAY

**18** THURSDAY

**19** FRIDAY

**20** SATURDAY

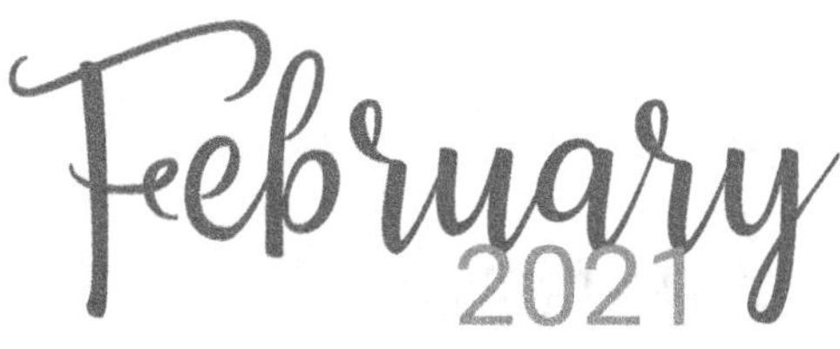

# February 2021

**21** SUNDAY

**22** MONDAY

**23** TUESDAY

**24** WEDNESDAY

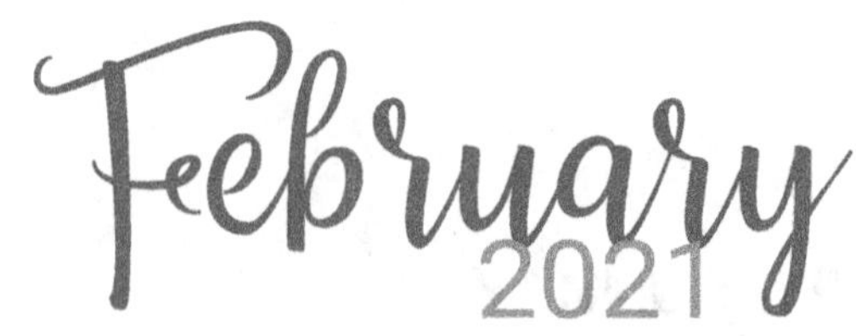


**25** THURSDAY

**26** FRIDAY

**27** SATURDAY

**28** SUNDAY

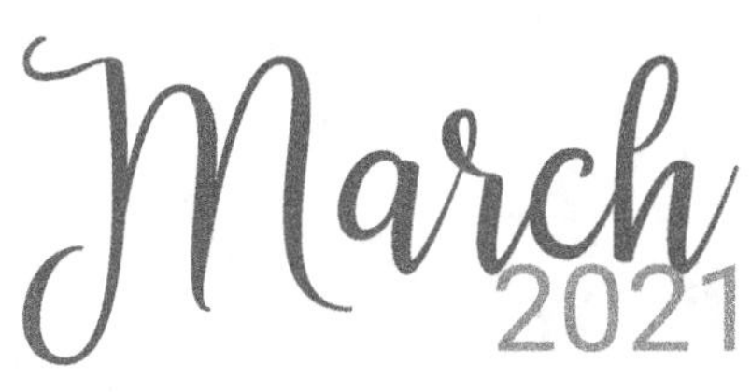


**01** MONDAY

**02** TUESDAY

**03** WEDNESDAY

**04** THURSDAY

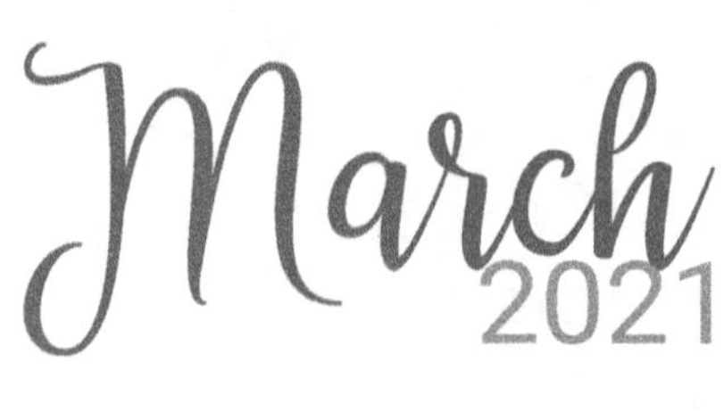

**05** FRIDAY

**06** SATURDAY

**07** SUNDAY

**08** MONDAY

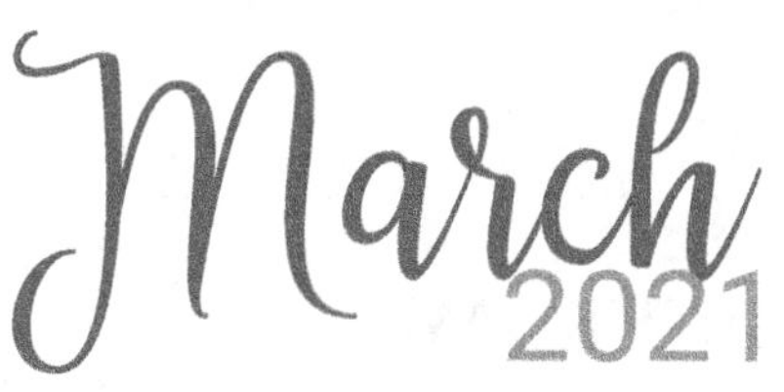


**09** TUESDAY

**10** WEDNESDAY

**11** THURSDAY

**12** FRIDAY

**13** SATURDAY

**14** SUNDAY

**15** MONDAY

**16** TUESDAY

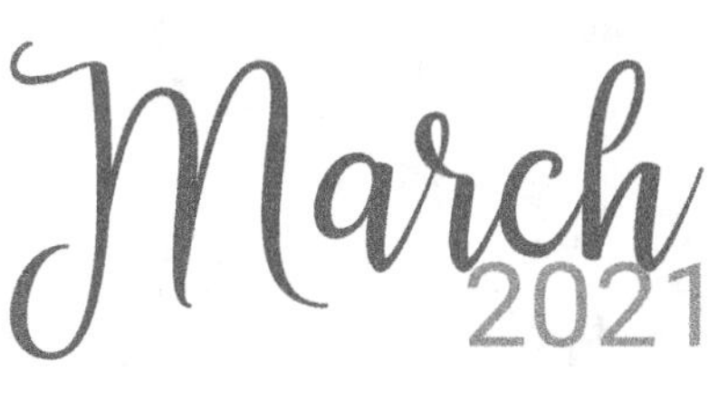


**17** WEDNESDAY

**18** THURSDAY

**19** FRIDAY

**20** SATURDAY

**March 2021**

**21** SUNDAY

**22** MONDAY

**23** TUESDAY

**24** WEDNESDAY

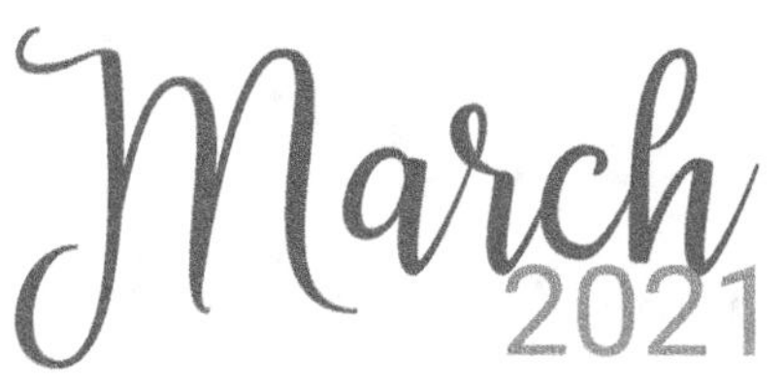

**25** THURSDAY

**26** FRIDAY

**27** SATURDAY

**28** SUNDAY

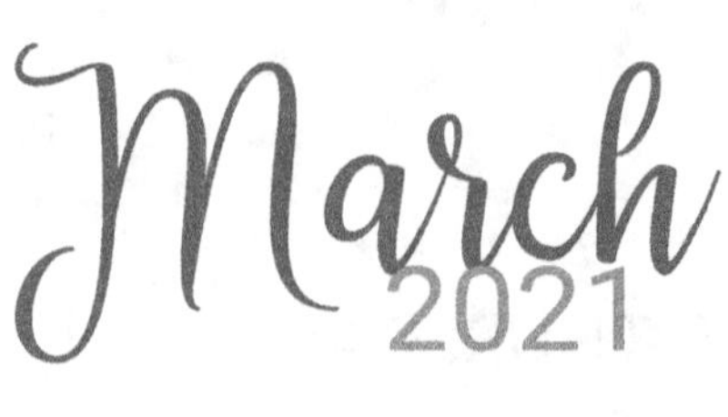

**29** MONDAY

**30** TUESDAY

**31** WEDNESDAY

NOTES

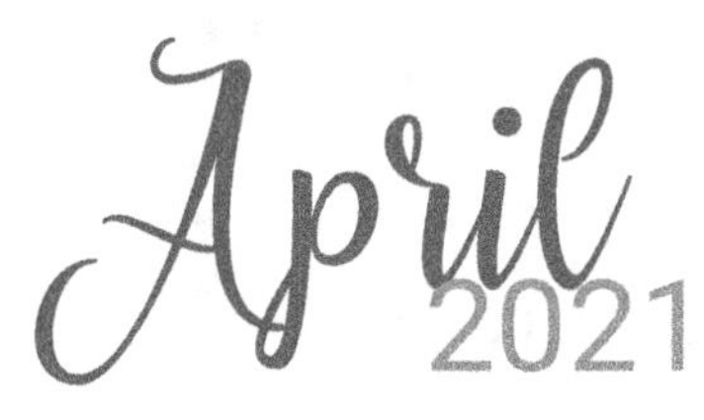

# April 2021

## 01 THURSDAY

## 02 FRIDAY

## 03 SATURDAY

## 04 SUNDAY

# April 2021

**05** MONDAY

**06** TUESDAY

**07** WEDNESDAY

**08** THURSDAY

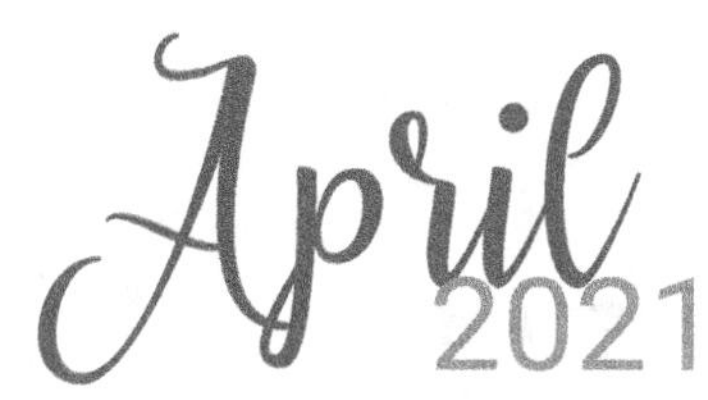

**09** FRIDAY

**10** SATURDAY

**11** SUNDAY

**12** MONDAY

## 13 TUESDAY

- 
- 
- 
- 
- 
- 
- 

## 14 WEDNESDAY

- 
- 
- 
- 
- 
- 
- 
- 

## 15 THURSDAY

- 
- 
- 
- 
- 
- 
- 
- 

## 16 FRIDAY

- 
- 
- 
- 
- 

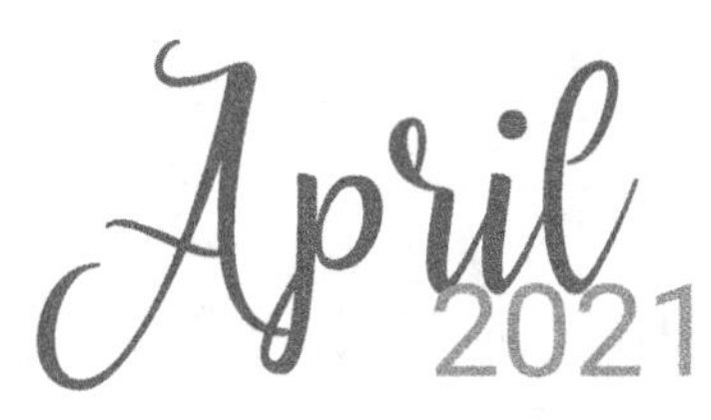


## 17 SATURDAY

## 18 SUNDAY

## 19 MONDAY

## 20 TUESDAY

**21** WEDNESDAY

**22** THURSDAY

**23** FRIDAY

**24** SATURDAY

**25** SUNDAY

**26** MONDAY

**27** TUESDAY

**28** WEDNESDAY

## 29 THURSDAY

## 30 FRIDAY

## NOTES

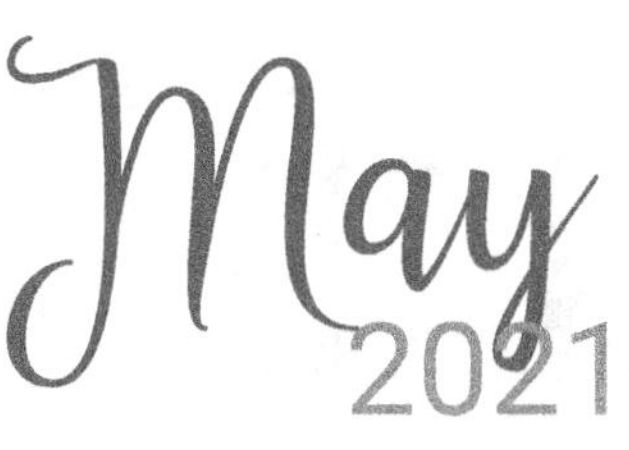

# May
## 2021

**01** SATURDAY

**02** SUNDAY

**03** MONDAY

**04** TUESDAY

**05** WEDNESDAY

**06** THURSDAY

**07** FRIDAY

**08** SATURDAY

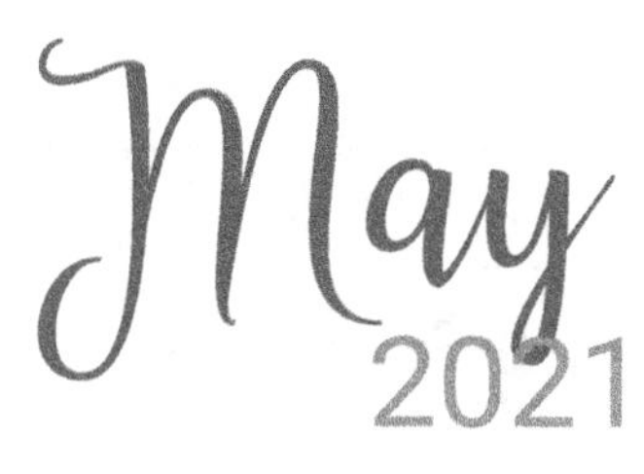


**09** SUNDAY

**10** MONDAY

**11** TUESDAY

**12** WEDNESDAY

**13** THURSDAY

**14** FRIDAY

**15** SATURDAY

**16** SUNDAY

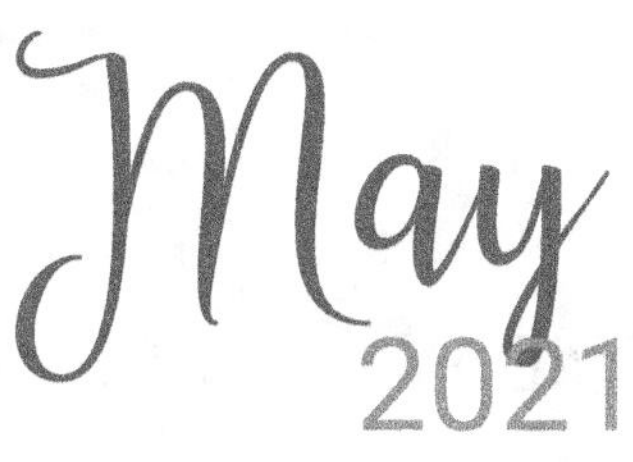



**17** MONDAY

**18** TUESDAY

**19** WEDNESDAY

**20** THURSDAY

# May
### 2021

**21** FRIDAY

**22** SATURDAY

**23** SUNDAY

**24** MONDAY

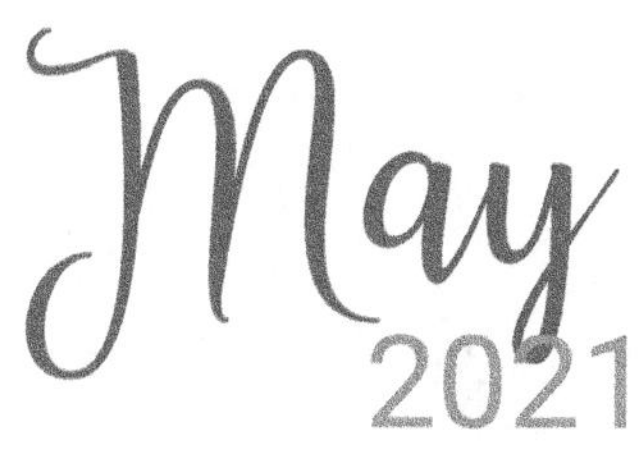


**25** TUESDAY

**26** WEDNESDAY

**27** THURSDAY

**28** FRIDAY

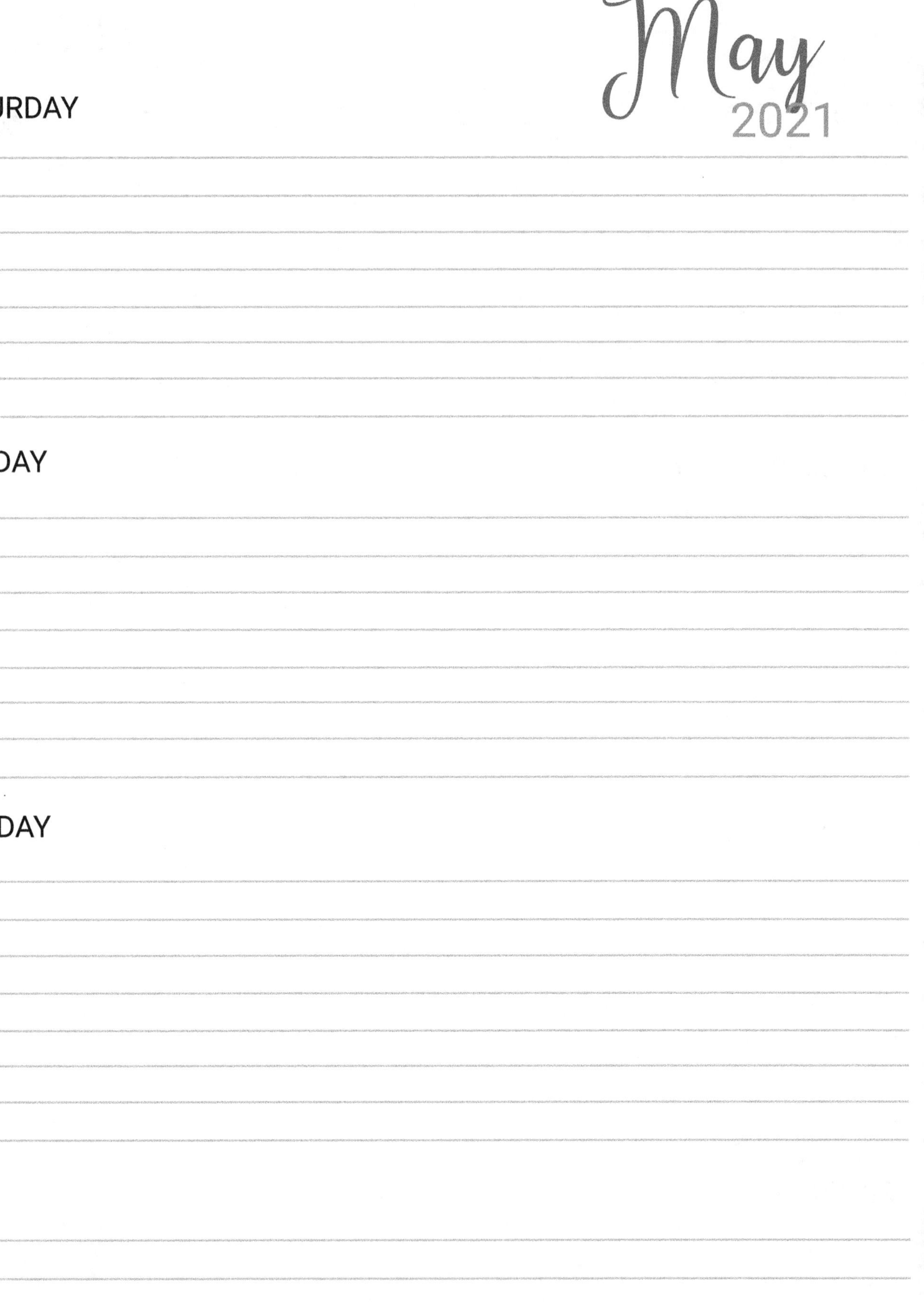


**29** SATURDAY

**30** SUNDAY

**31** MONDAY

NOTES

**01** TUESDAY

**02** WEDNESDAY

**03** THURSDAY

**04** FRIDAY

# June 2021

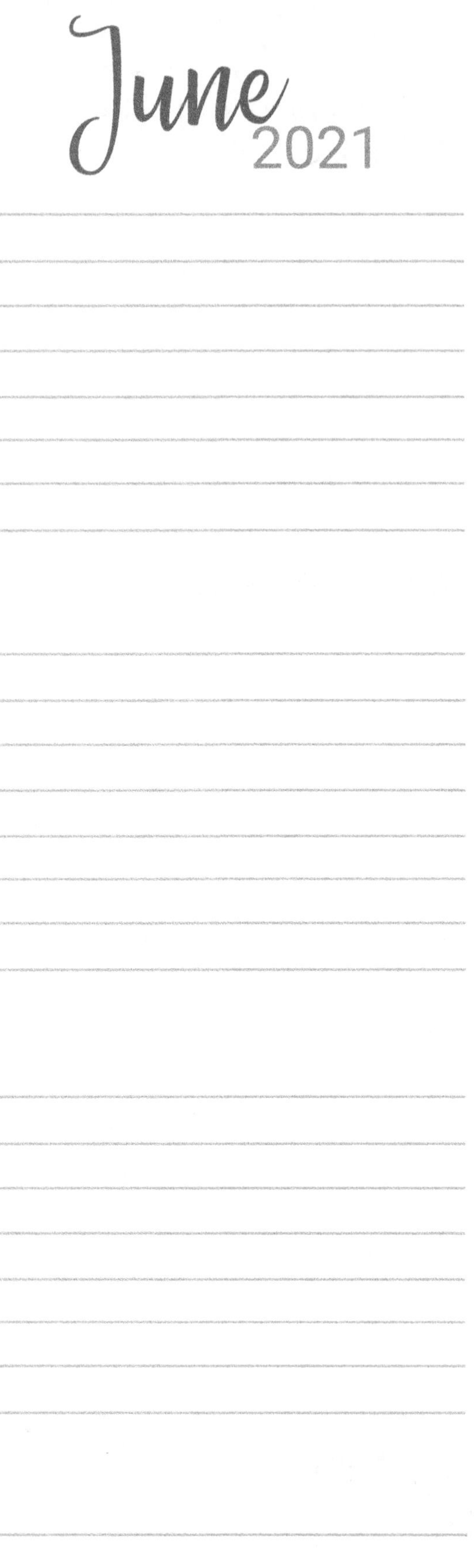

**05** SATURDAY

**06** SUNDAY

**07** MONDAY

**08** TUESDAY

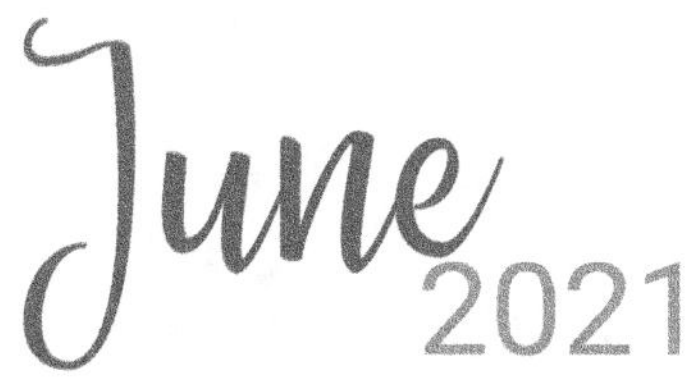

**09** WEDNESDAY

**10** THURSDAY

**11** FRIDAY

**12** SATURDAY

**13** SUNDAY

**14** MONDAY

**15** TUESDAY

**16** WEDNESDAY

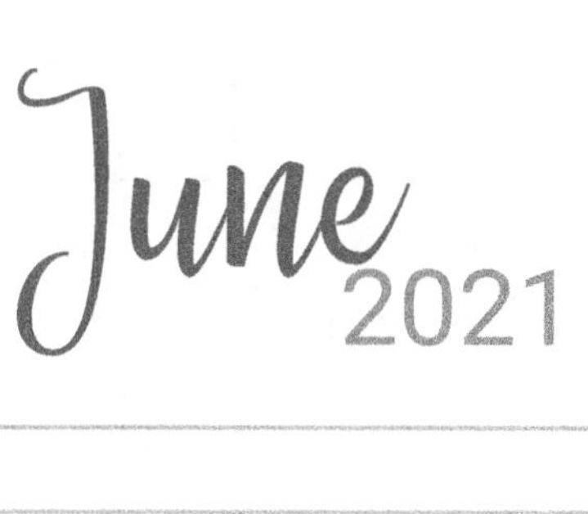



## 17 THURSDAY

## 18 FRIDAY

## 19 SATURDAY

## 20 SUNDAY

**21** MONDAY

○
○
○
○
○
○
○
○

**22** TUESDAY

○
○
○
○
○
○
○
○

**23** WEDNESDAY

○
○
○
○
○
○
○
○

**24** THURSDAY

○
○
○
○
○

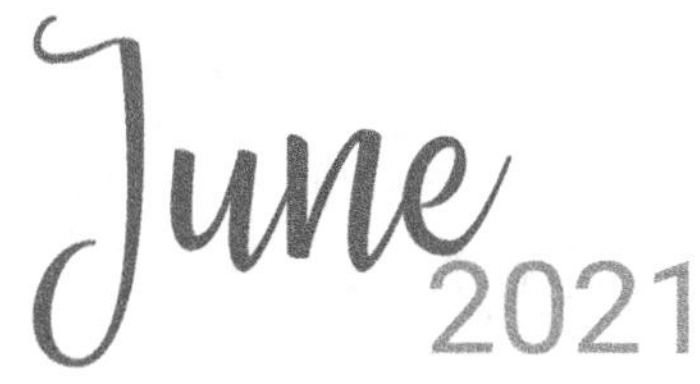


**25** FRIDAY

**26** SATURDAY

**27** SUNDAY

**28** MONDAY

## 29 TUESDAY

○
○
○
○
○
○
○
○

## 30 WEDNESDAY

○
○
○
○
○
○
○
○

## NOTES

**01** THURSDAY

**02** FRIDAY

**03** SATURDAY

**04** SUNDAY

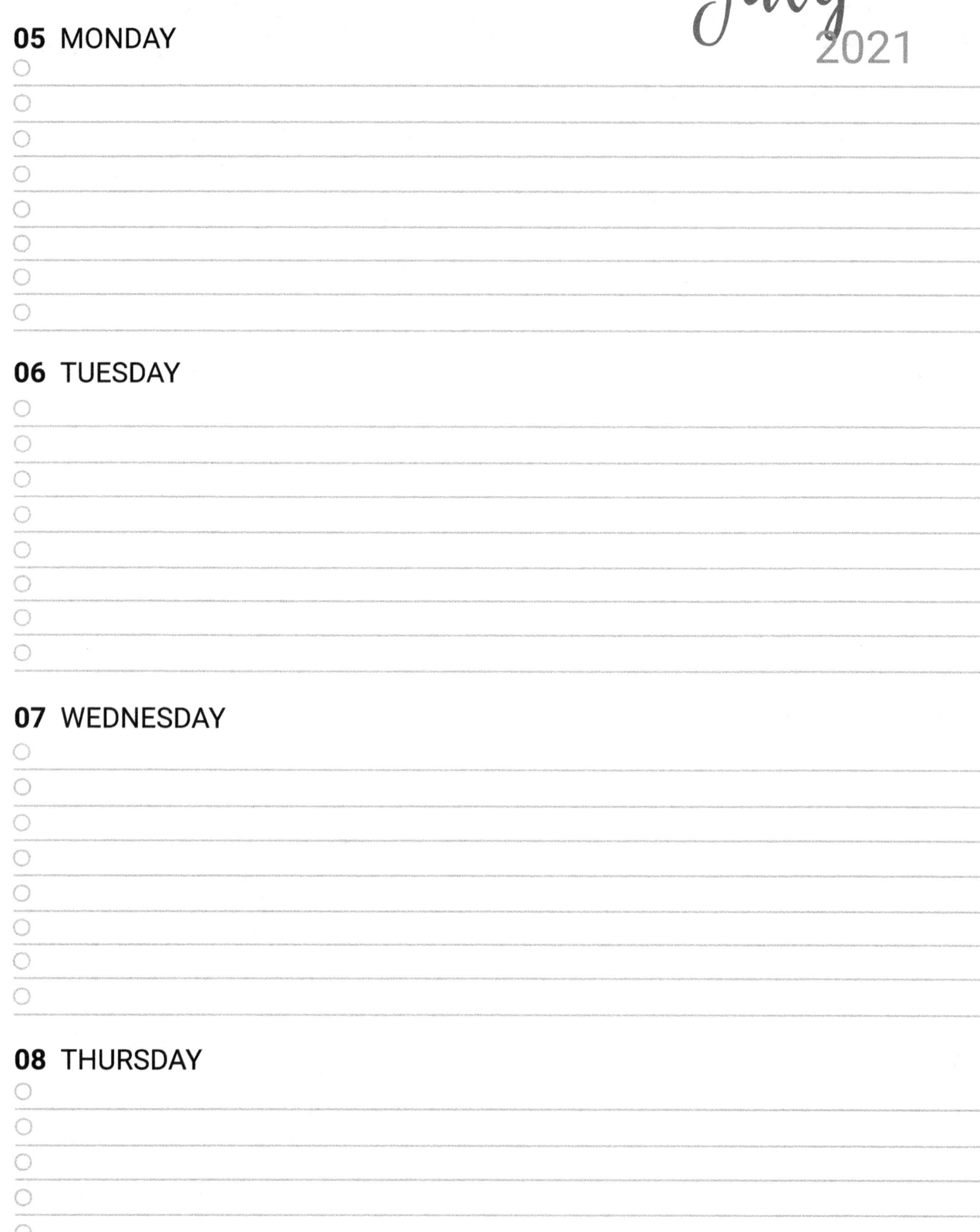


July
2021

05 MONDAY

06 TUESDAY

07 WEDNESDAY

08 THURSDAY

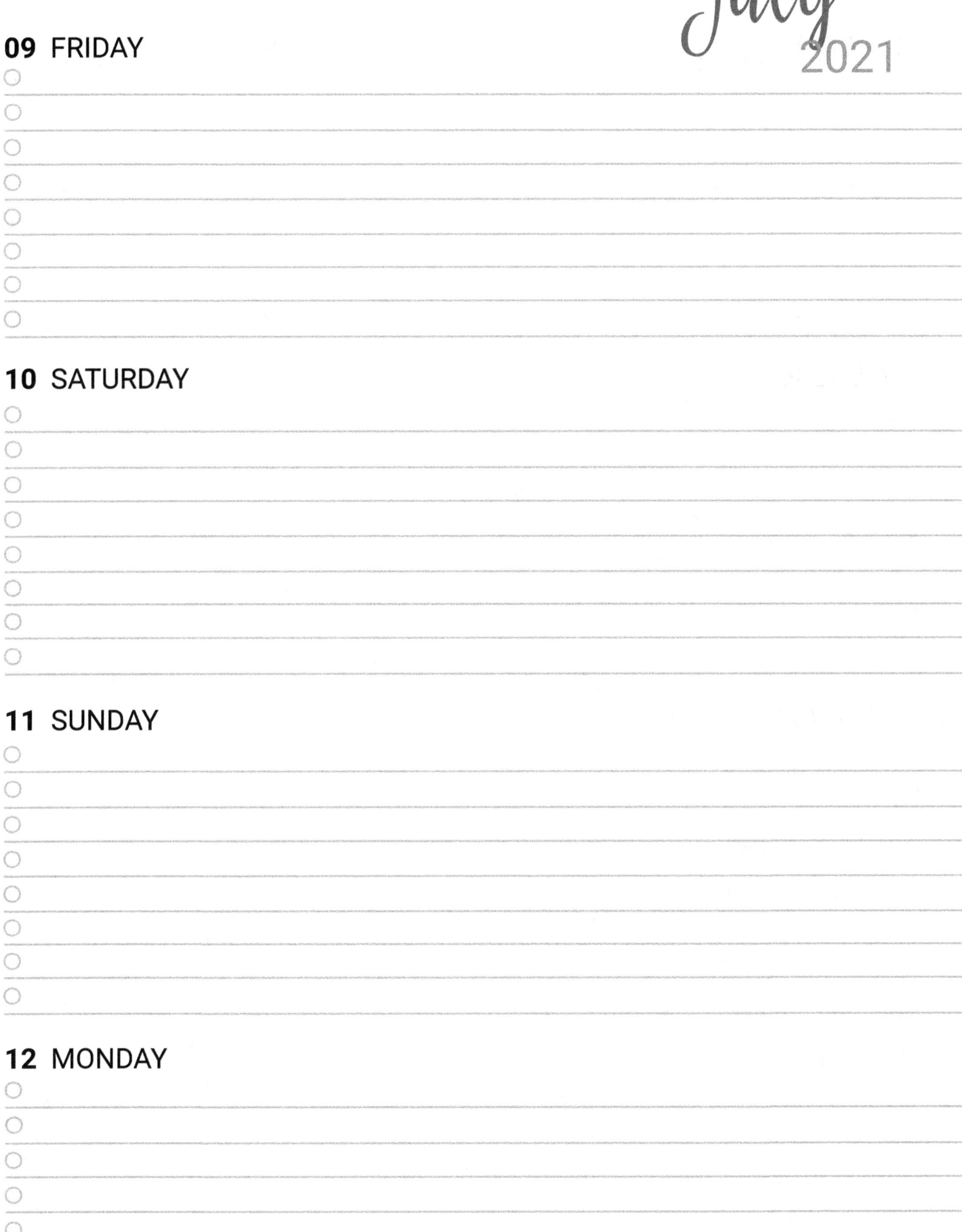

**09** FRIDAY

**10** SATURDAY

**11** SUNDAY

**12** MONDAY

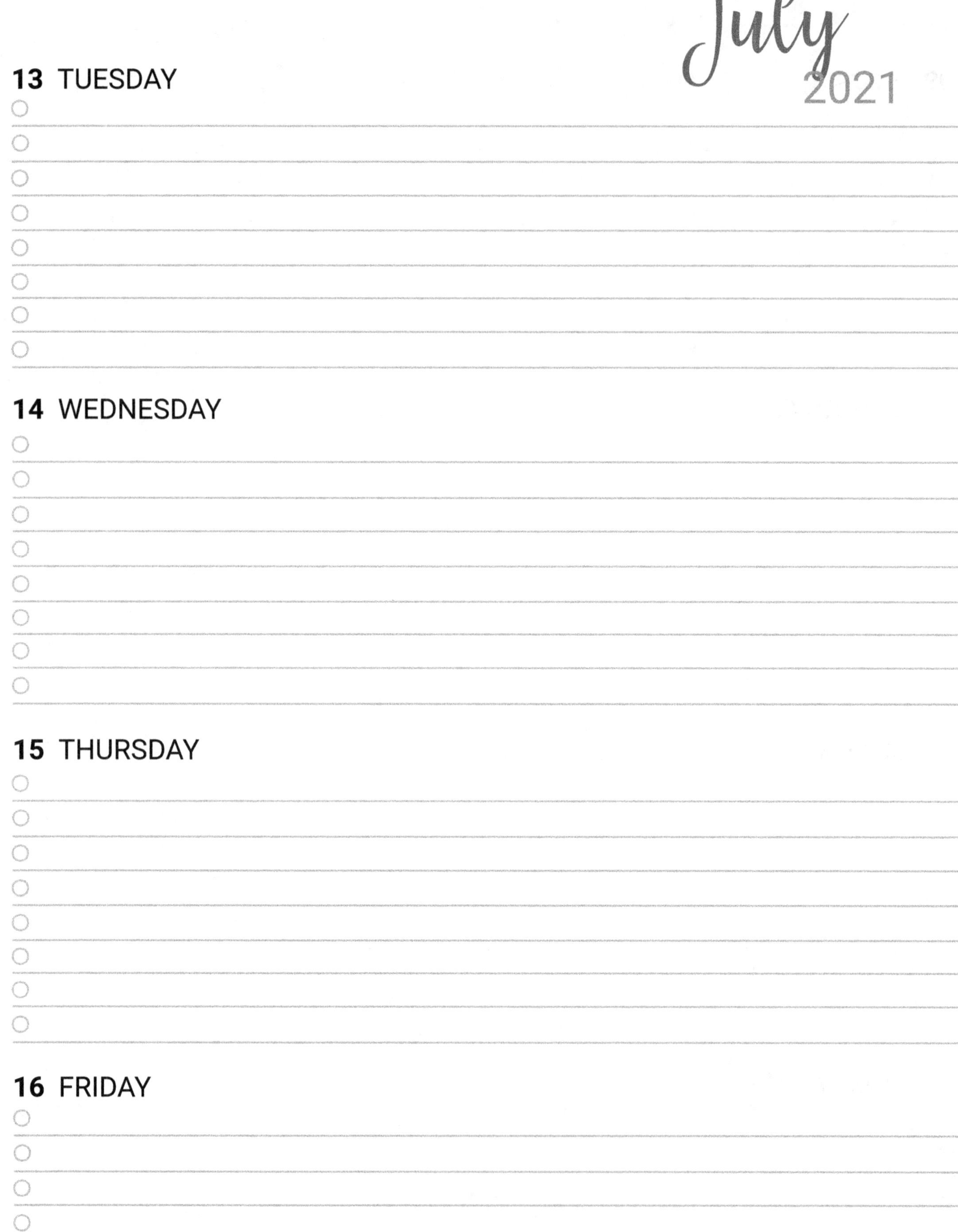

**13** TUESDAY

**14** WEDNESDAY

**15** THURSDAY

**16** FRIDAY

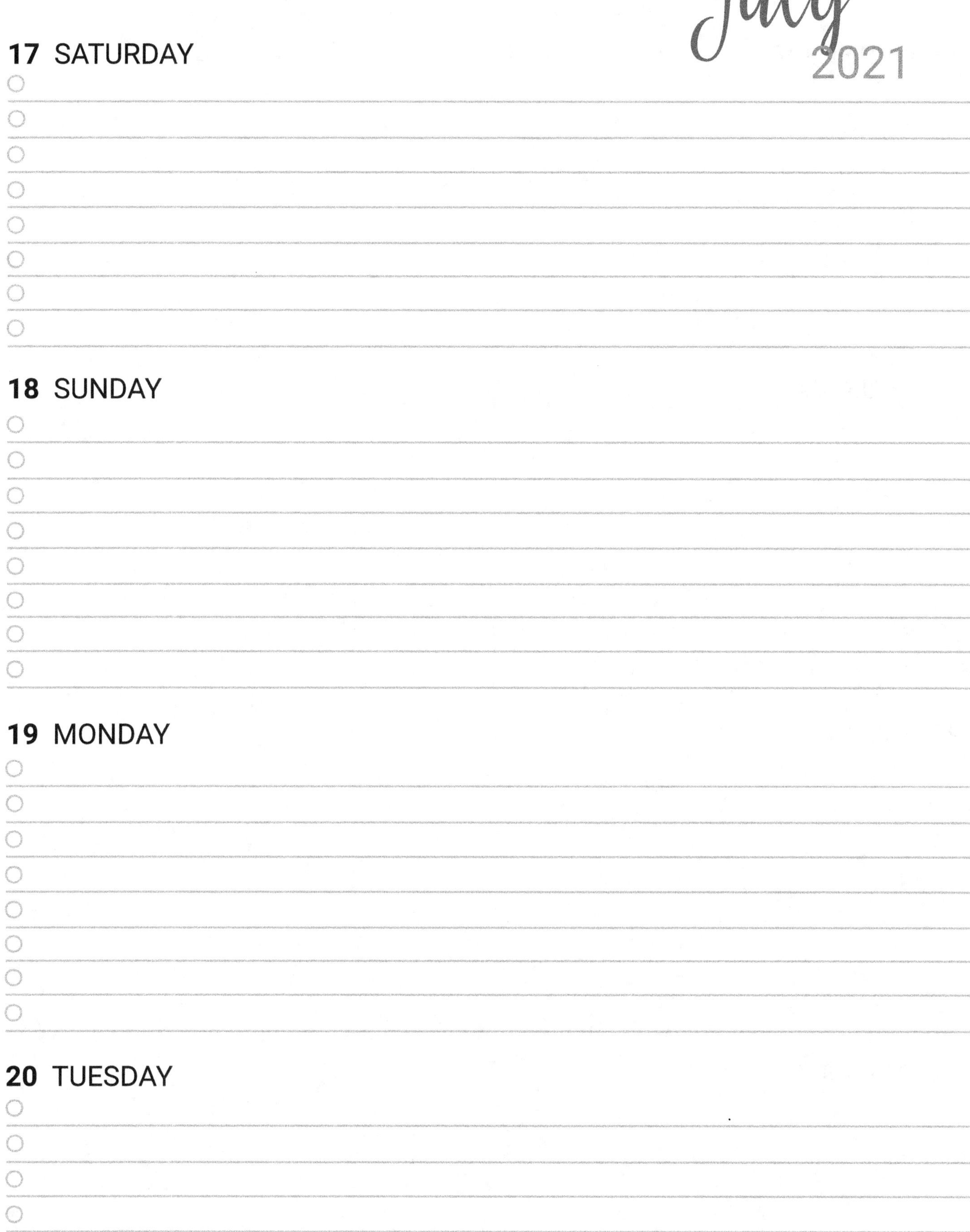



**17** SATURDAY

**18** SUNDAY

**19** MONDAY

**20** TUESDAY

**21** WEDNESDAY

**22** THURSDAY

**23** FRIDAY

**24** SATURDAY

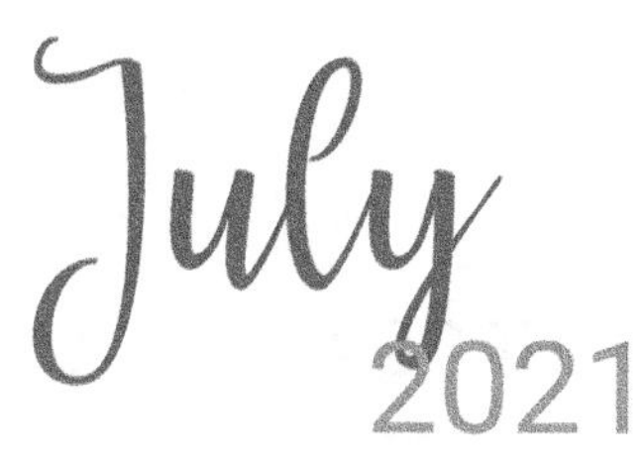


**25** SUNDAY

**26** MONDAY

**27** TUESDAY

**28** WEDNESDAY

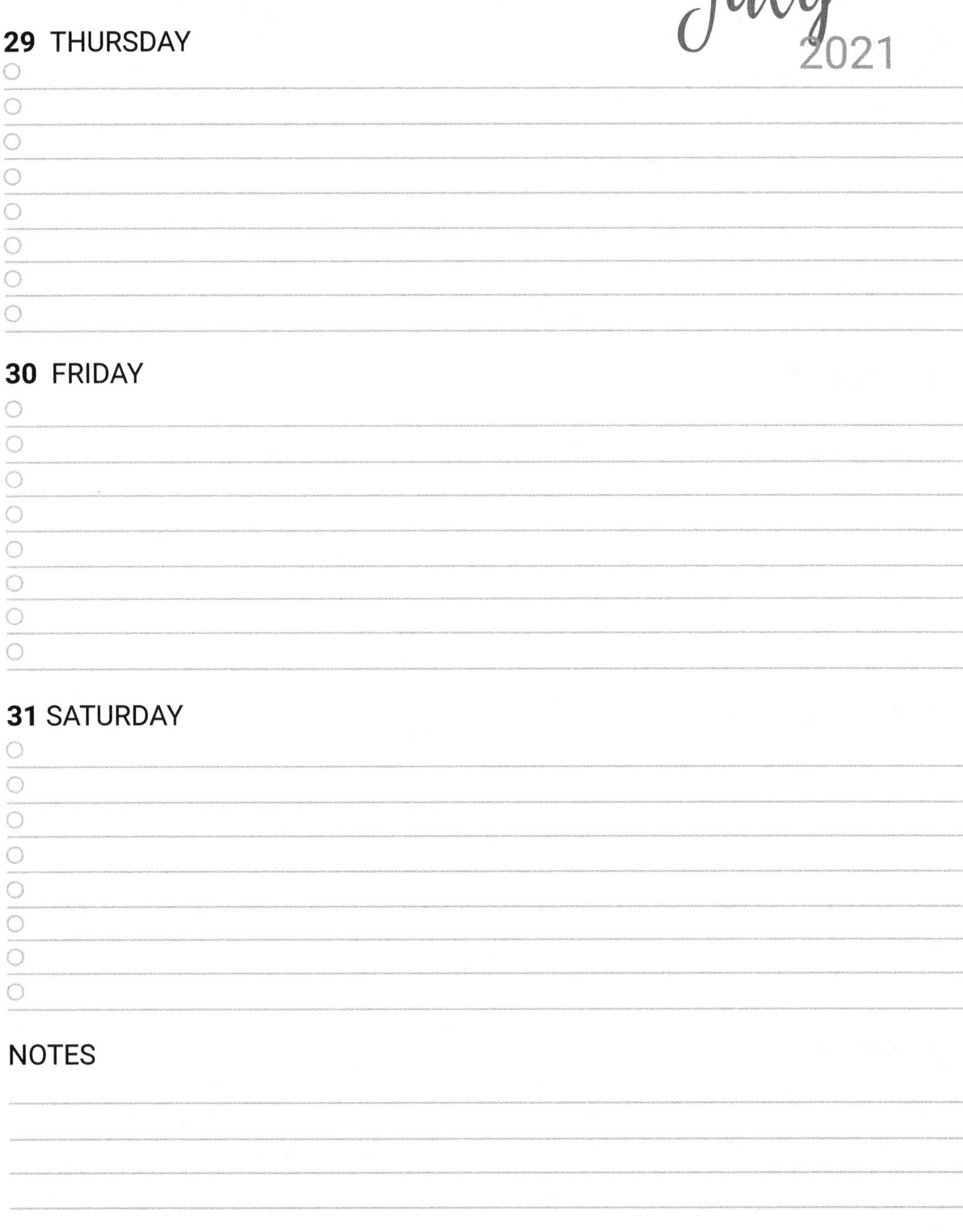


July
2021

**29** THURSDAY

**30** FRIDAY

**31** SATURDAY

NOTES

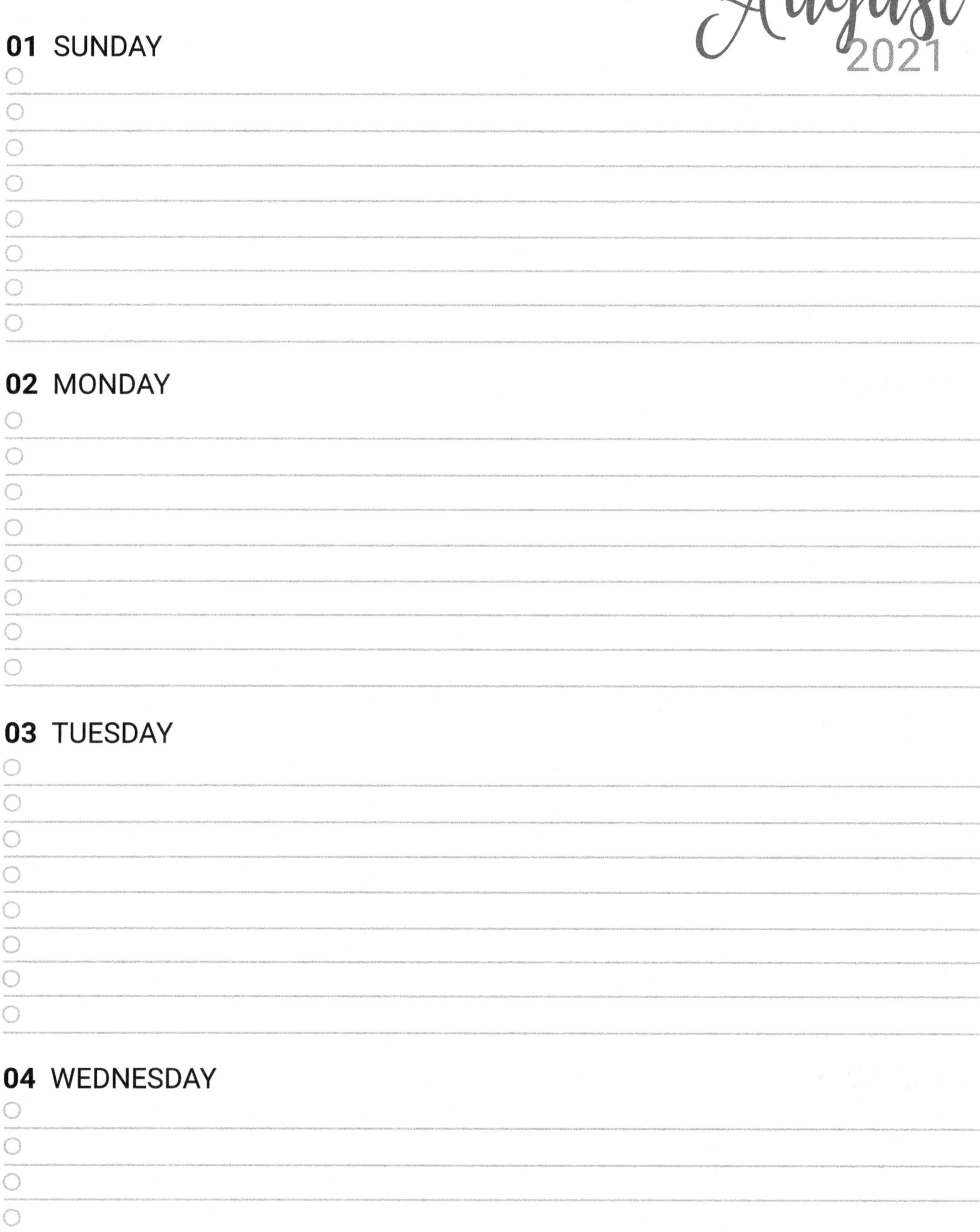


August
2021
01 SUNDAY
02 MONDAY
03 TUESDAY
04 WEDNESDAY

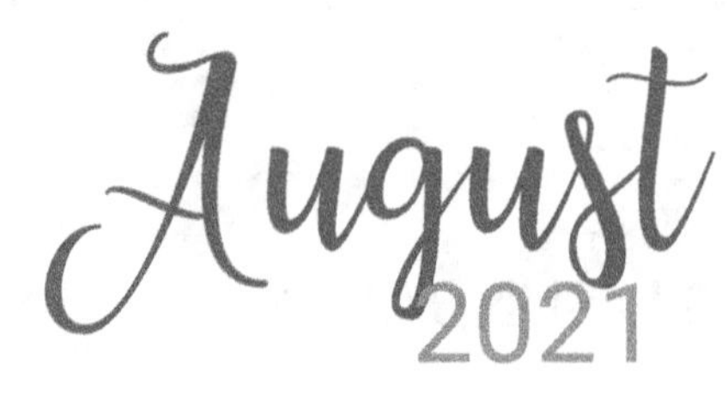


**05** THURSDAY

**06** FRIDAY

**07** SATURDAY

**08** SUNDAY

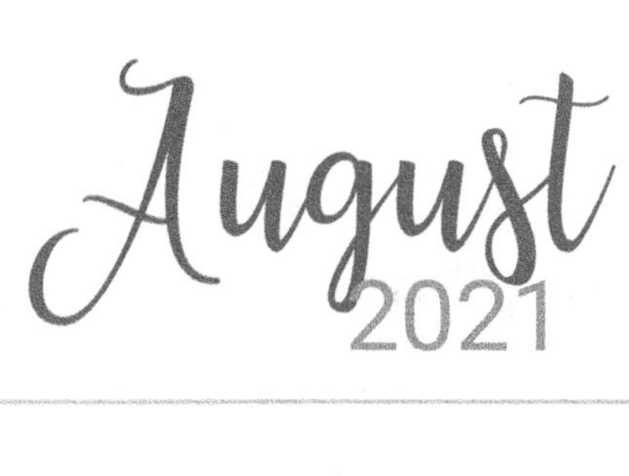


**09** MONDAY

**10** TUESDAY

**11** WEDNESDAY

**12** THURSDAY

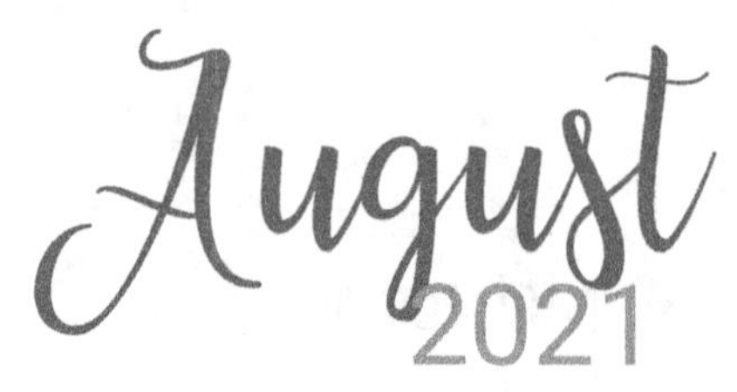

# August
## 2021

**13** FRIDAY

**14** SATURDAY

**15** SUNDAY

**16** MONDAY

**17** TUESDAY

**18** WEDNESDAY

**19** THURSDAY

**20** FRIDAY

**21** SATURDAY

**22** SUNDAY

**23** MONDAY

**24** TUESDAY

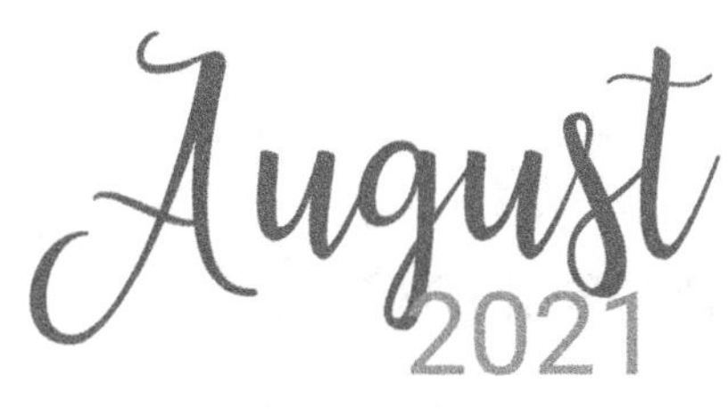

# August 2021

**25** WEDNESDAY

**26** THURSDAY

**27** FRIDAY

**28** SATURDAY

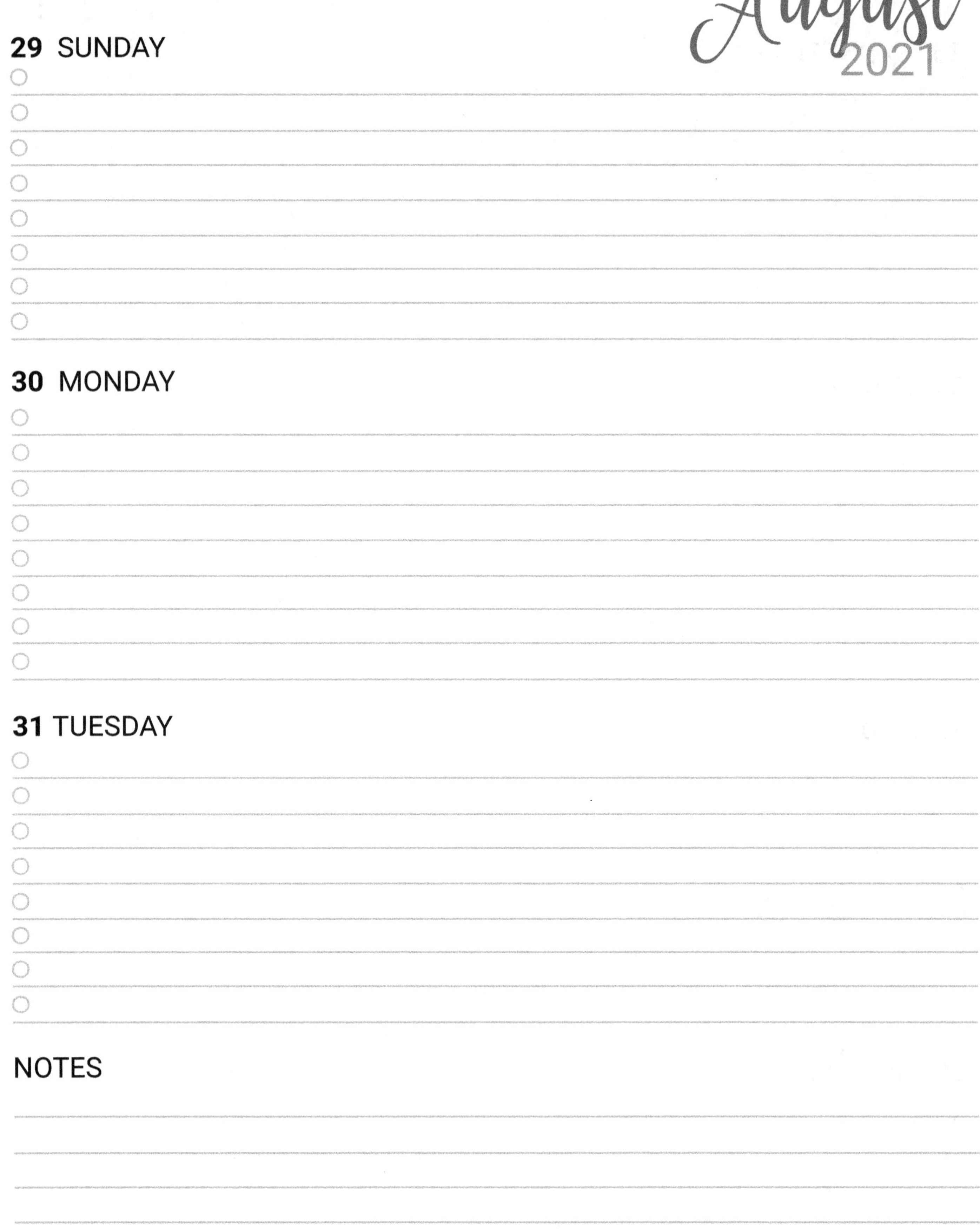



**29** SUNDAY

**30** MONDAY

**31** TUESDAY

NOTES

*September*<br>2021

**01** WEDNESDAY

**02** THURSDAY

**03** FRIDAY

**04** SATURDAY

**05** SUNDAY

**06** MONDAY

**07** TUESDAY

**08** WEDNESDAY

# September 2021

**09** THURSDAY

**10** FRIDAY

**11** SATURDAY

**12** SUNDAY

**13** MONDAY

**14** TUESDAY

**15** WEDNESDAY

**16** THURSDAY

**17** FRIDAY

**18** SATURDAY

**19** SUNDAY

**20** MONDAY

**21** TUESDAY

**22** WEDNESDAY

**23** THURSDAY

**24** FRIDAY

**25** SATURDAY

○
○
○
○
○
○
○
○

**26** SUNDAY

○
○
○
○
○
○
○
○

**27** MONDAY

○
○
○
○
○
○
○
○

**28** TUESDAY

○
○
○
○
○

**29** WEDNESDAY

**30** THURSDAY

NOTES

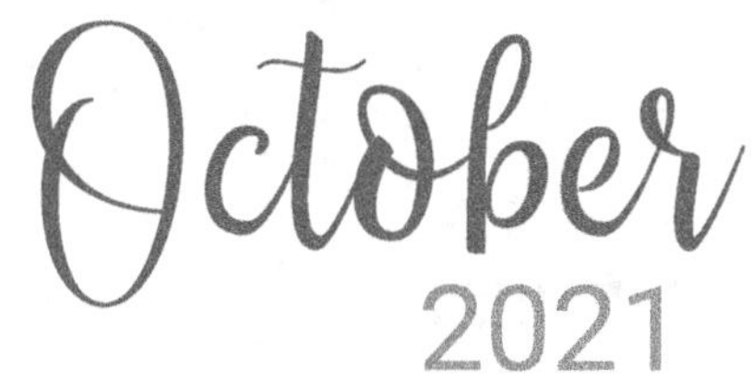

# October
## 2021

**01** FRIDAY

**02** SATURDAY

**03** SUNDAY

**04** MONDAY

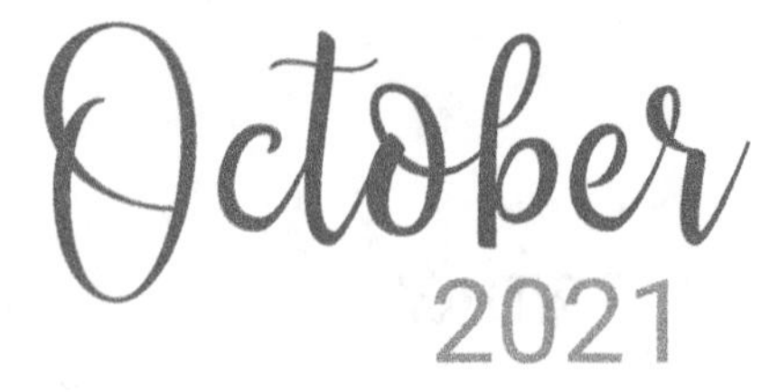


## 05 TUESDAY

## 06 WEDNESDAY

## 07 THURSDAY

## 08 FRIDAY

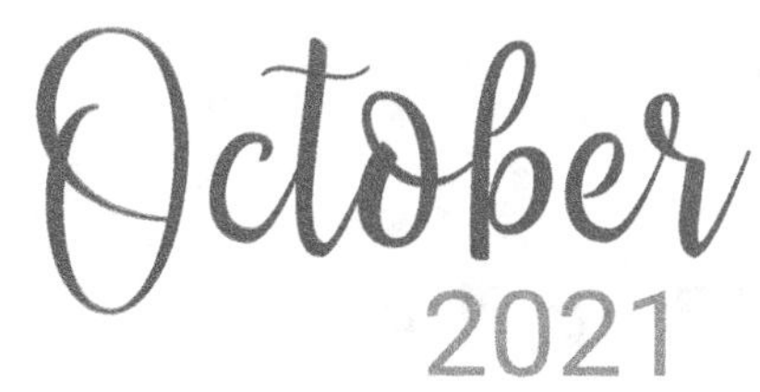



**09** SATURDAY

**10** SUNDAY

**11** MONDAY

**12** TUESDAY

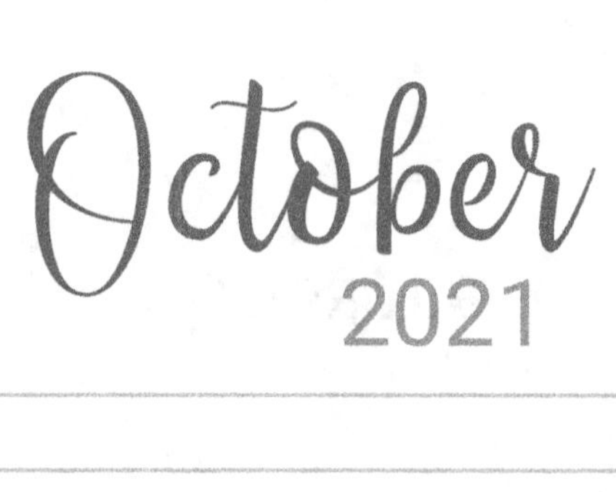

October
2021

## 13 WEDNESDAY

## 14 THURSDAY

## 15 FRIDAY

## 16 SATURDAY

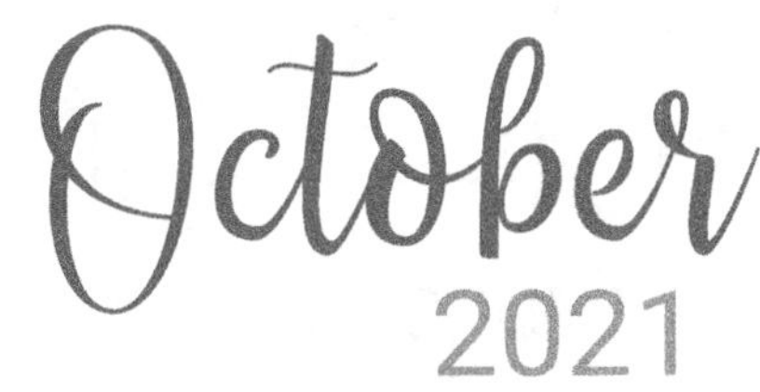



**17** SUNDAY

**18** MONDAY

**19** TUESDAY

**20** WEDNESDAY

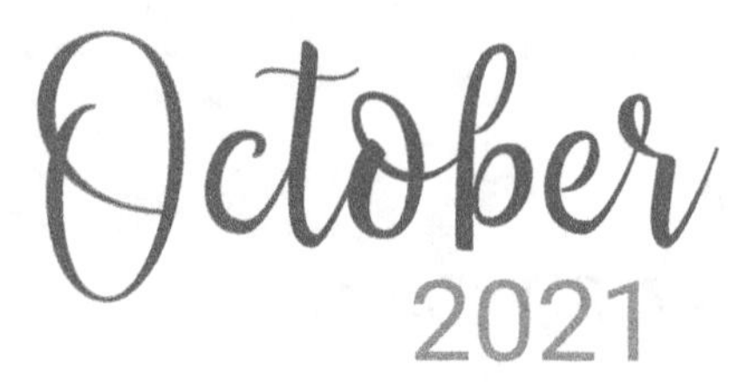


**21** THURSDAY

**22** FRIDAY

**23** SATURDAY

**24** SUNDAY

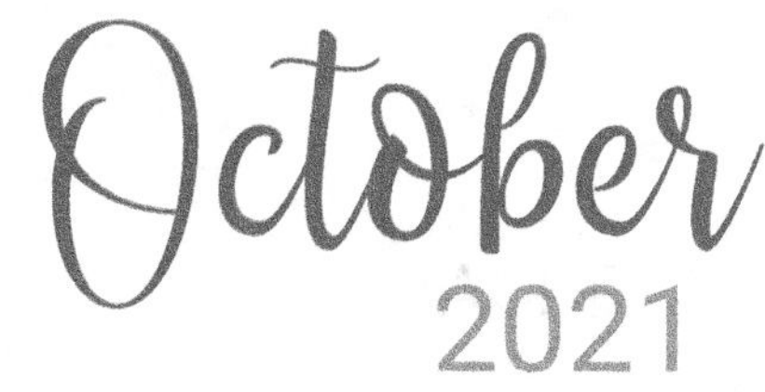


**25** MONDAY

**26** TUESDAY

**27** WEDNESDAY

**28** THURSDAY

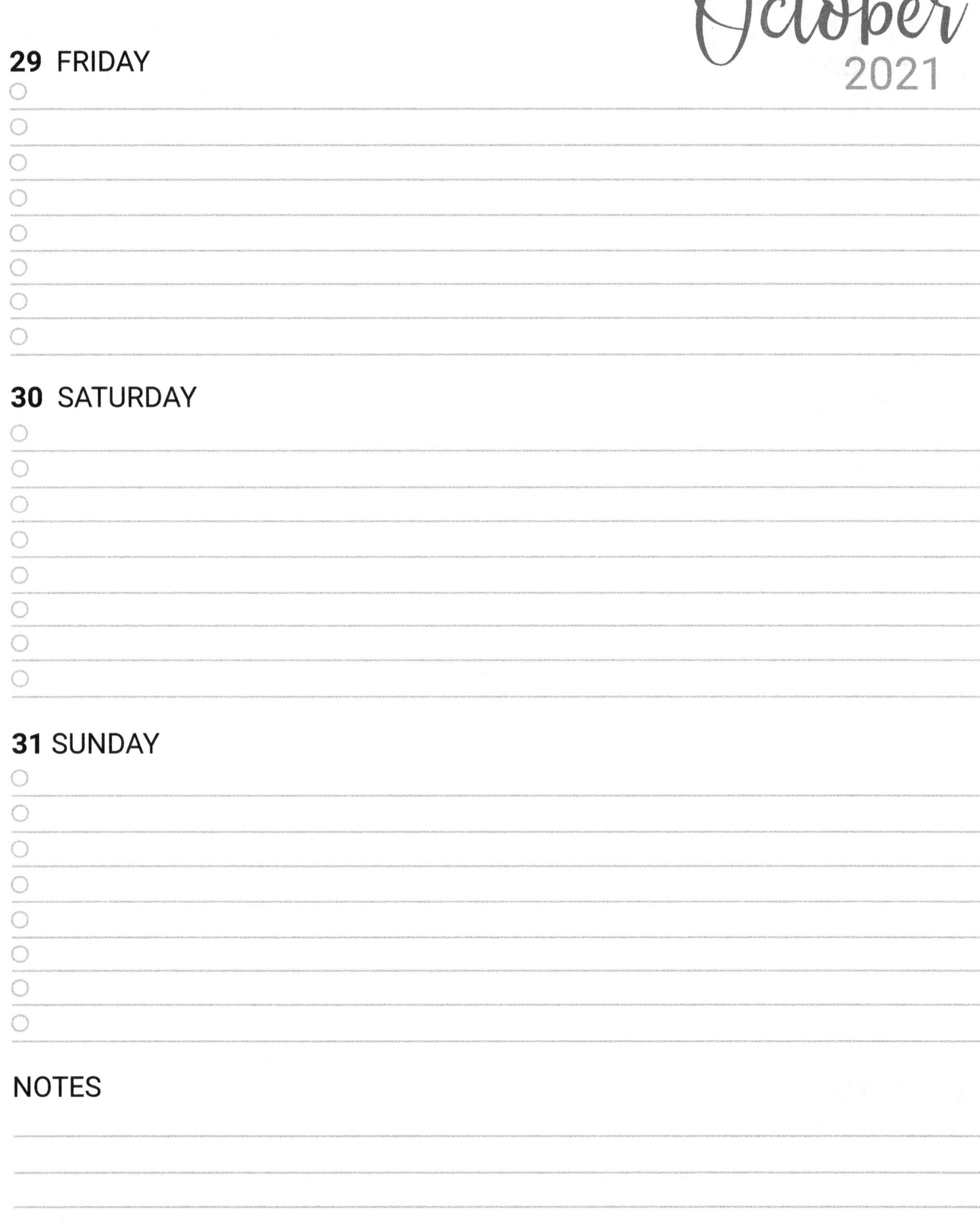

# October
## 2021

**29** FRIDAY

**30** SATURDAY

**31** SUNDAY

NOTES

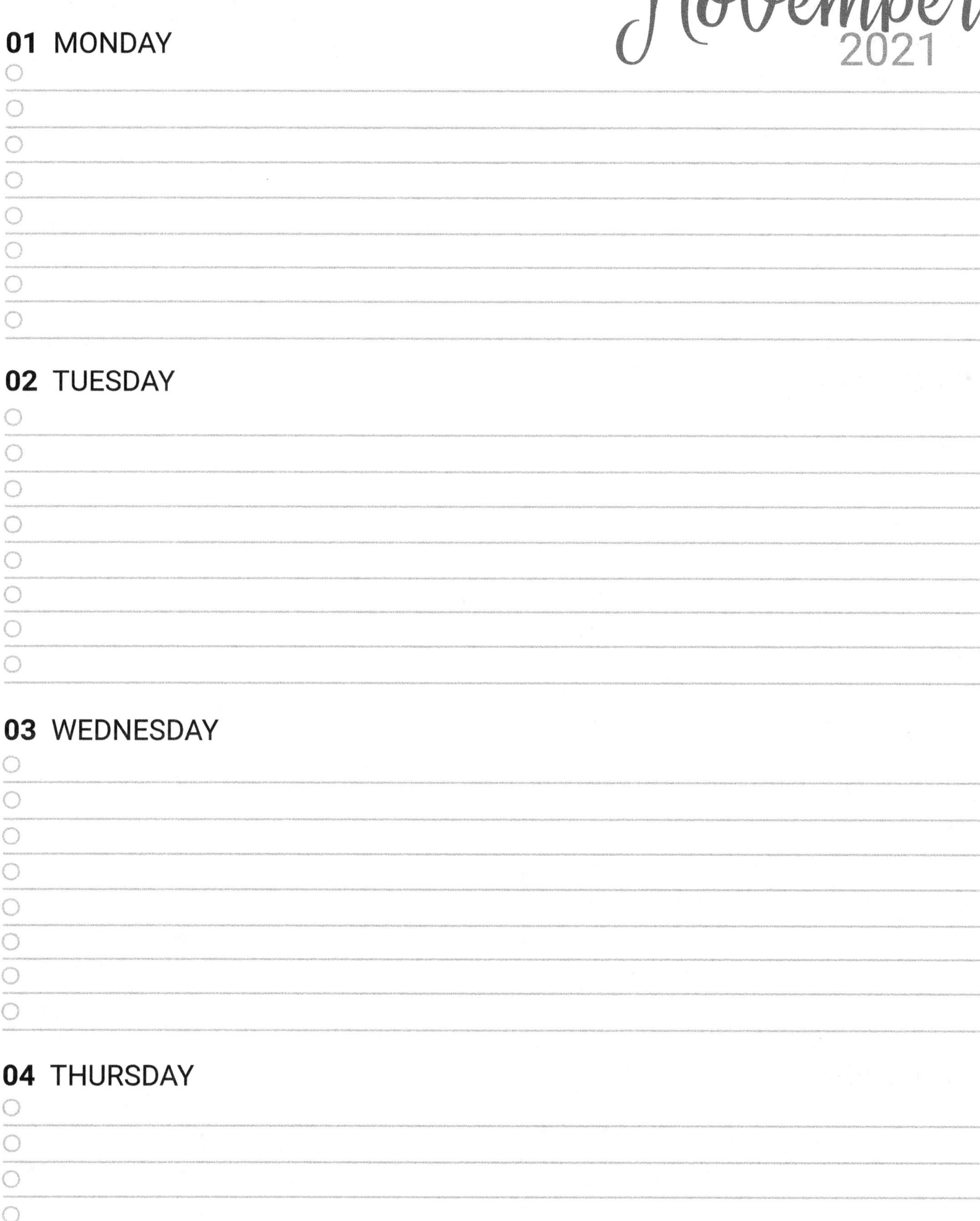



**01** MONDAY

**02** TUESDAY

**03** WEDNESDAY

**04** THURSDAY

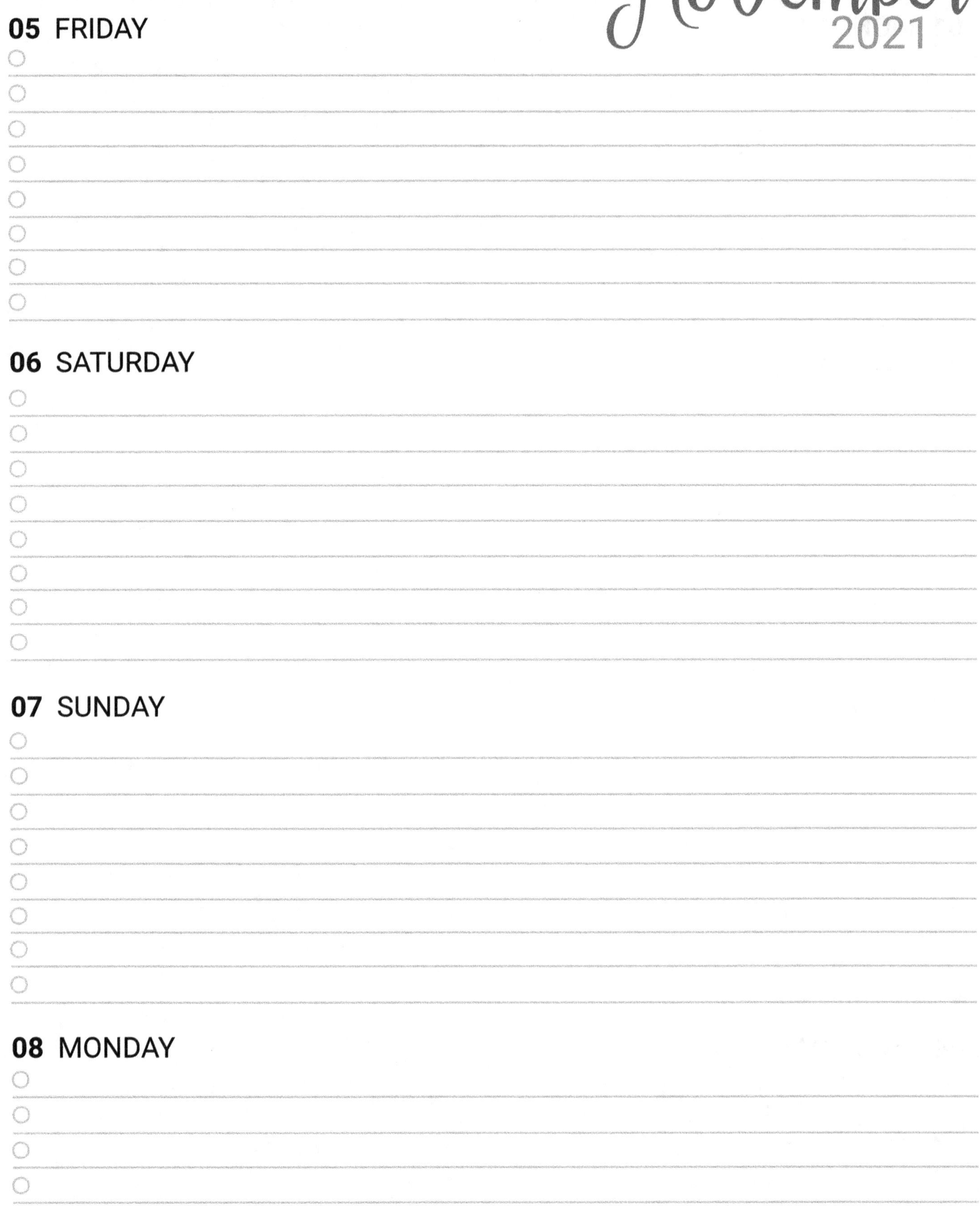



**05** FRIDAY

**06** SATURDAY

**07** SUNDAY

**08** MONDAY

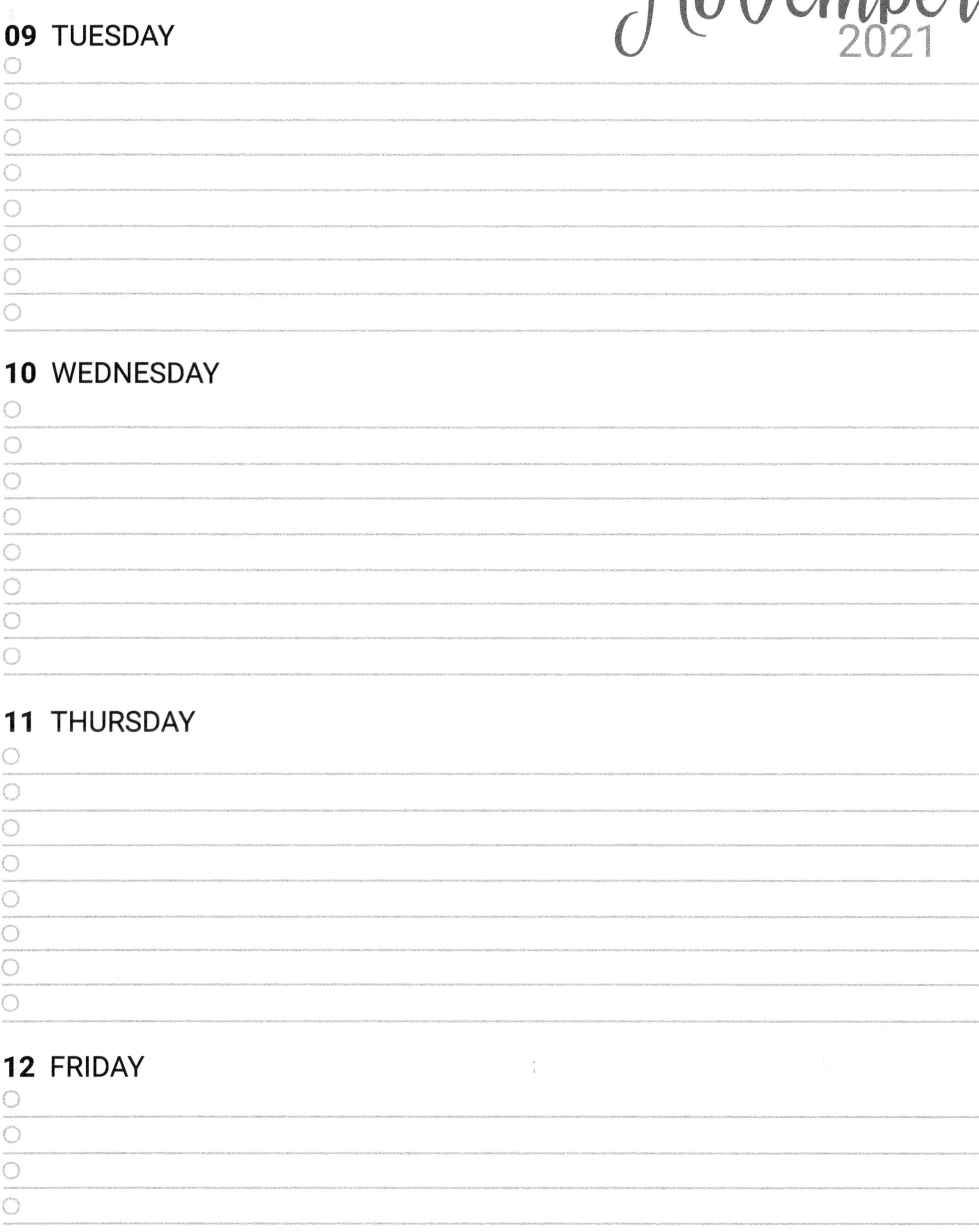



**09** TUESDAY

**10** WEDNESDAY

**11** THURSDAY

**12** FRIDAY

**13** SATURDAY

**14** SUNDAY

**15** MONDAY

**16** TUESDAY

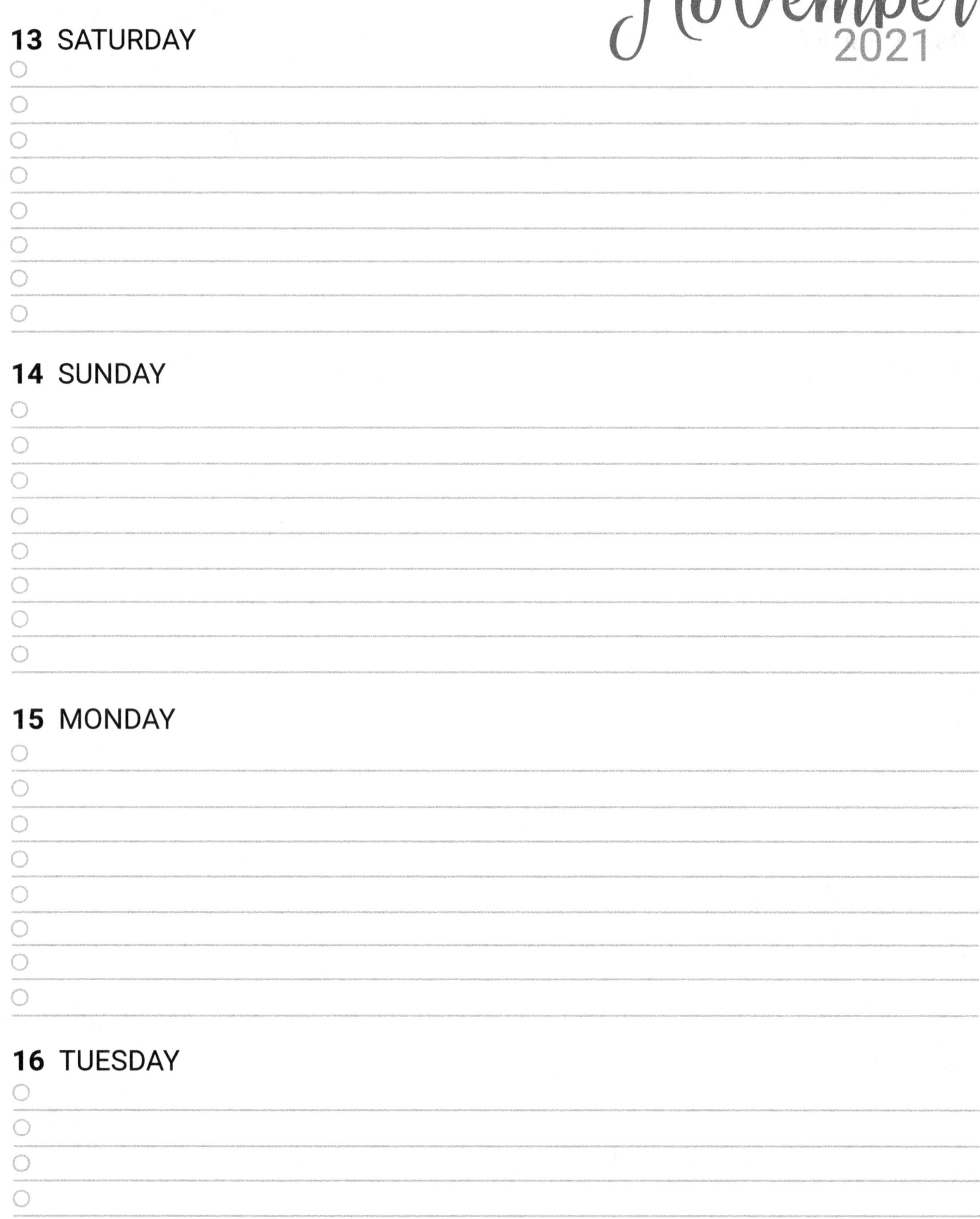

**17** WEDNESDAY

**18** THURSDAY

**19** FRIDAY

**20** SATURDAY

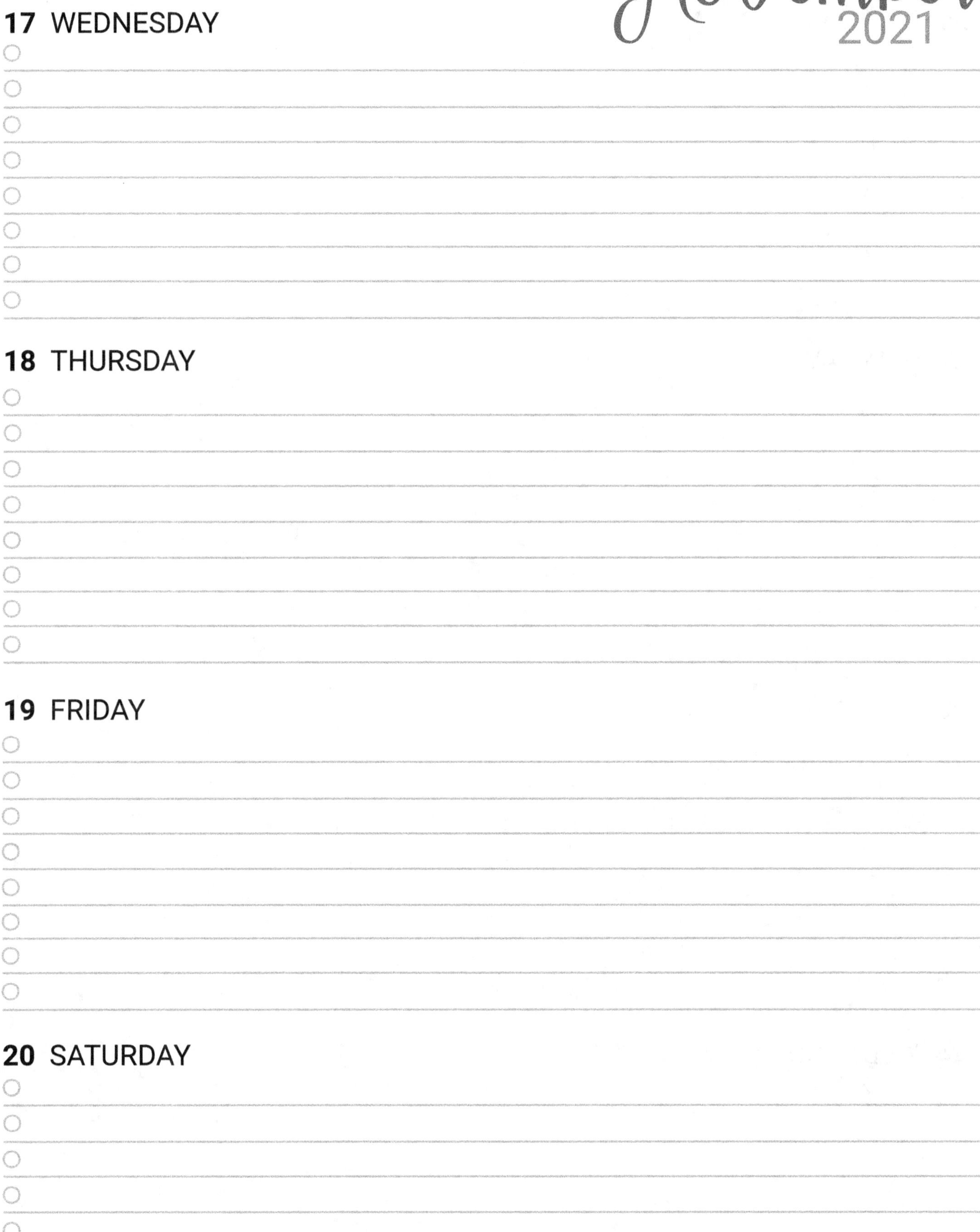

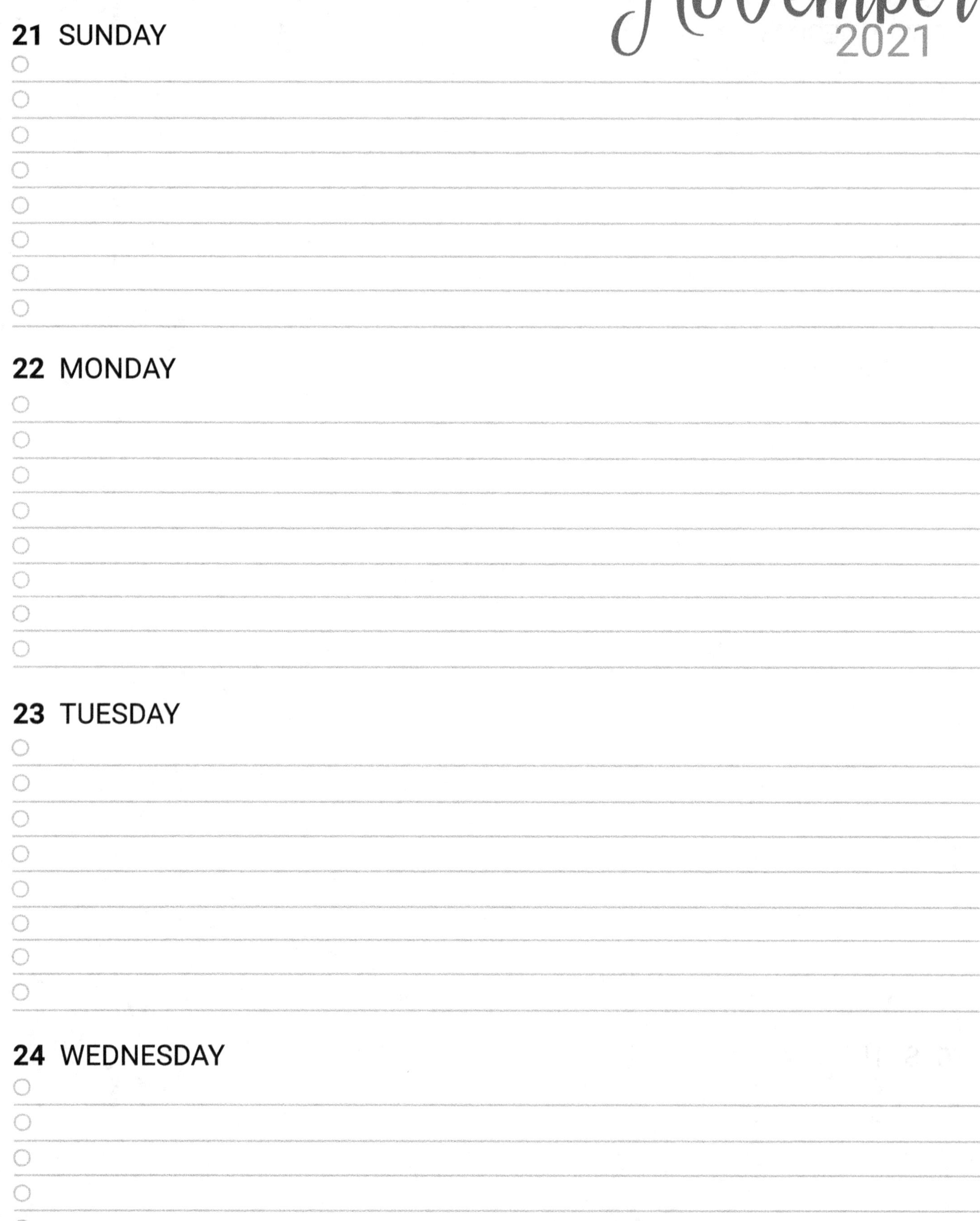


November
2021

**21** SUNDAY

**22** MONDAY

**23** TUESDAY

**24** WEDNESDAY

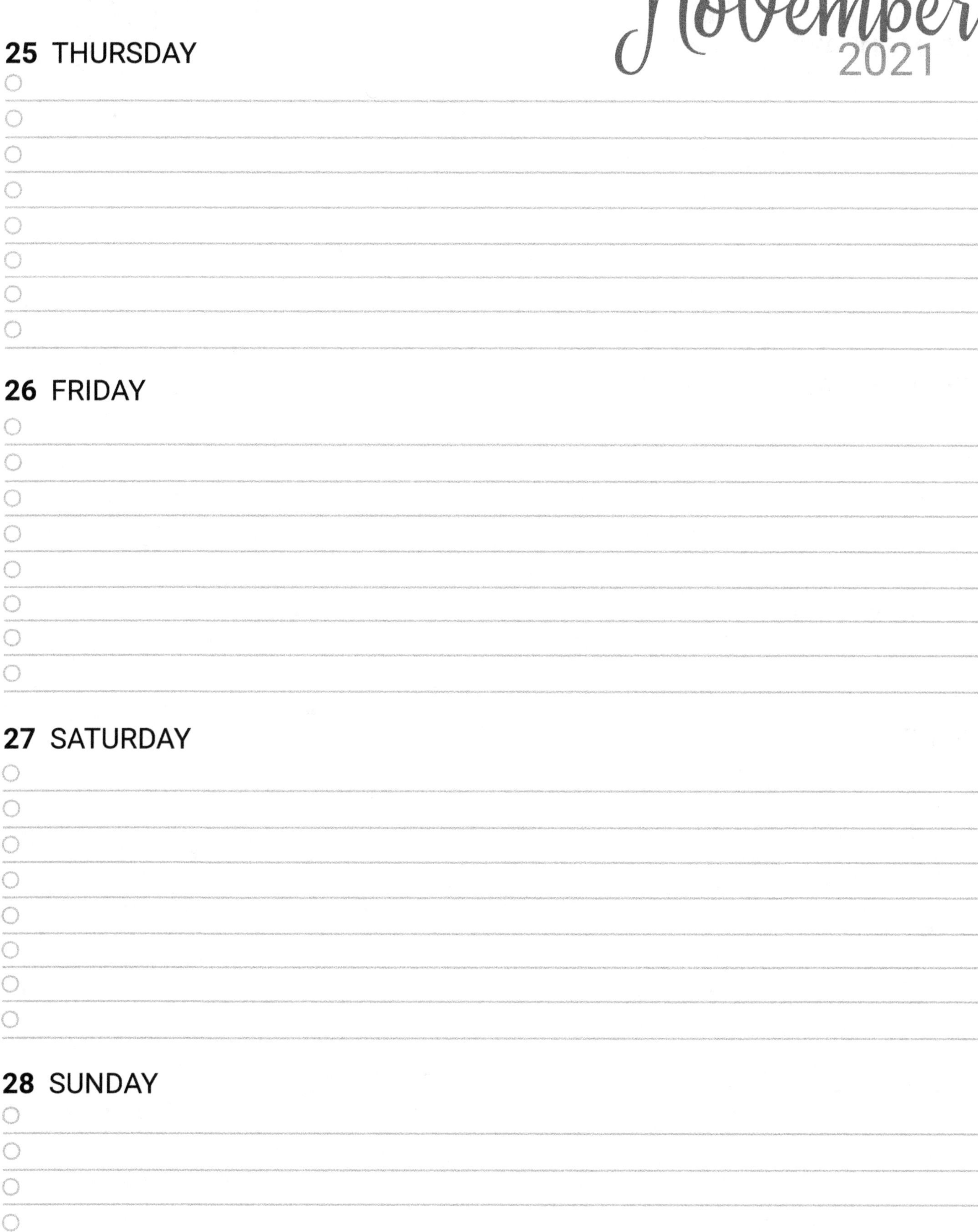


November
2021

25 THURSDAY

26 FRIDAY

27 SATURDAY

28 SUNDAY

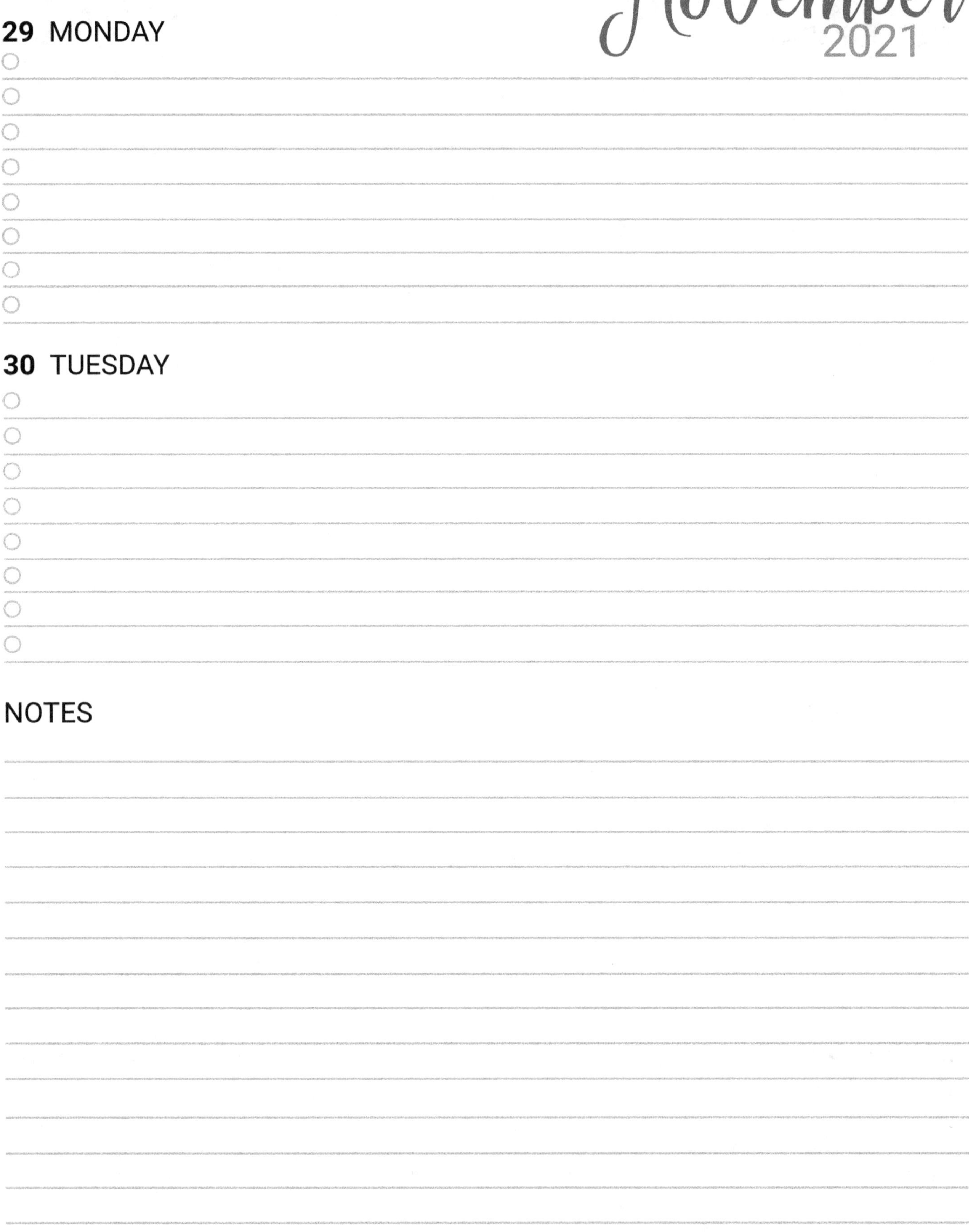


November
2021

29 MONDAY

30 TUESDAY

NOTES

**01** WEDNESDAY

**02** THURSDAY

**03** FRIDAY

**04** SATURDAY

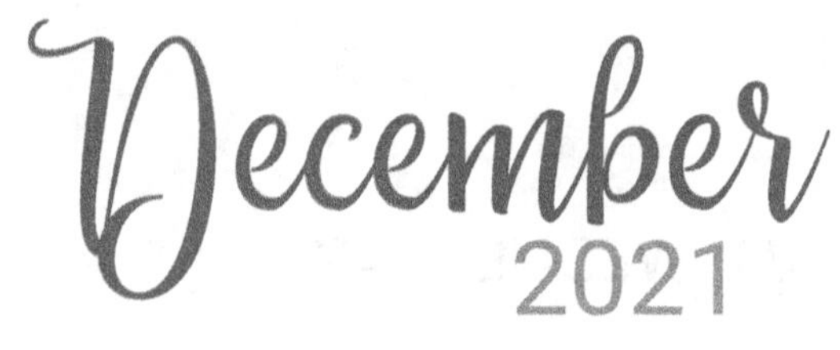


**05** SUNDAY

**06** MONDAY

**07** TUESDAY

**08** WEDNESDAY

**09** THURSDAY

**10** FRIDAY

**11** SATURDAY

**12** SUNDAY

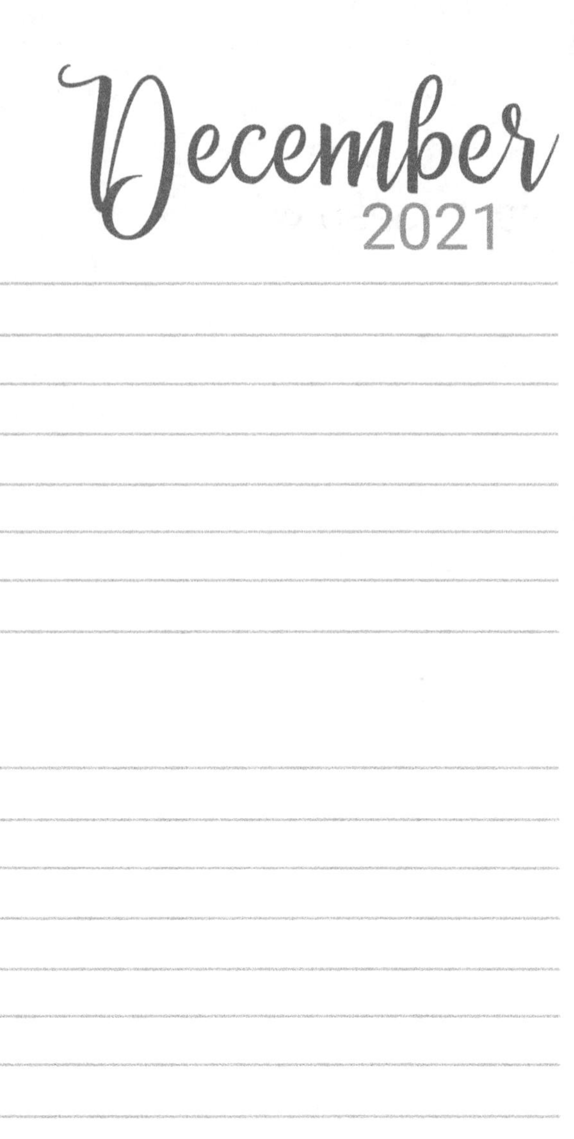


**13** MONDAY

**14** TUESDAY

**15** WEDNESDAY

**16** THURSDAY

# December
## 2021

**17** FRIDAY

**18** SATURDAY

**19** SUNDAY

**20** MONDAY

**21** TUESDAY

**22** WEDNESDAY

**23** THURSDAY

**24** FRIDAY

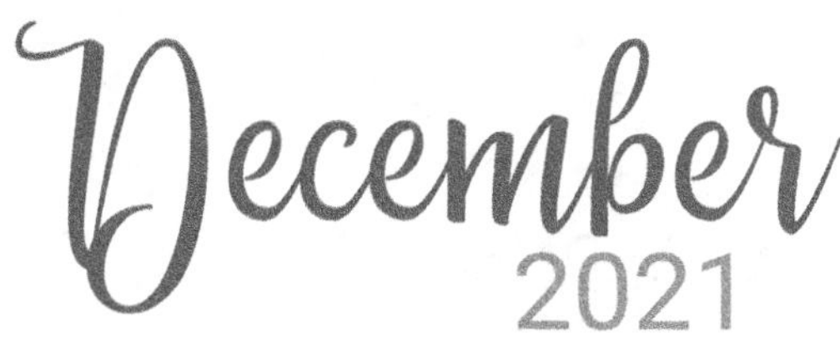



**25** SATURDAY

**26** SUNDAY

**27** MONDAY

**28** TUESDAY

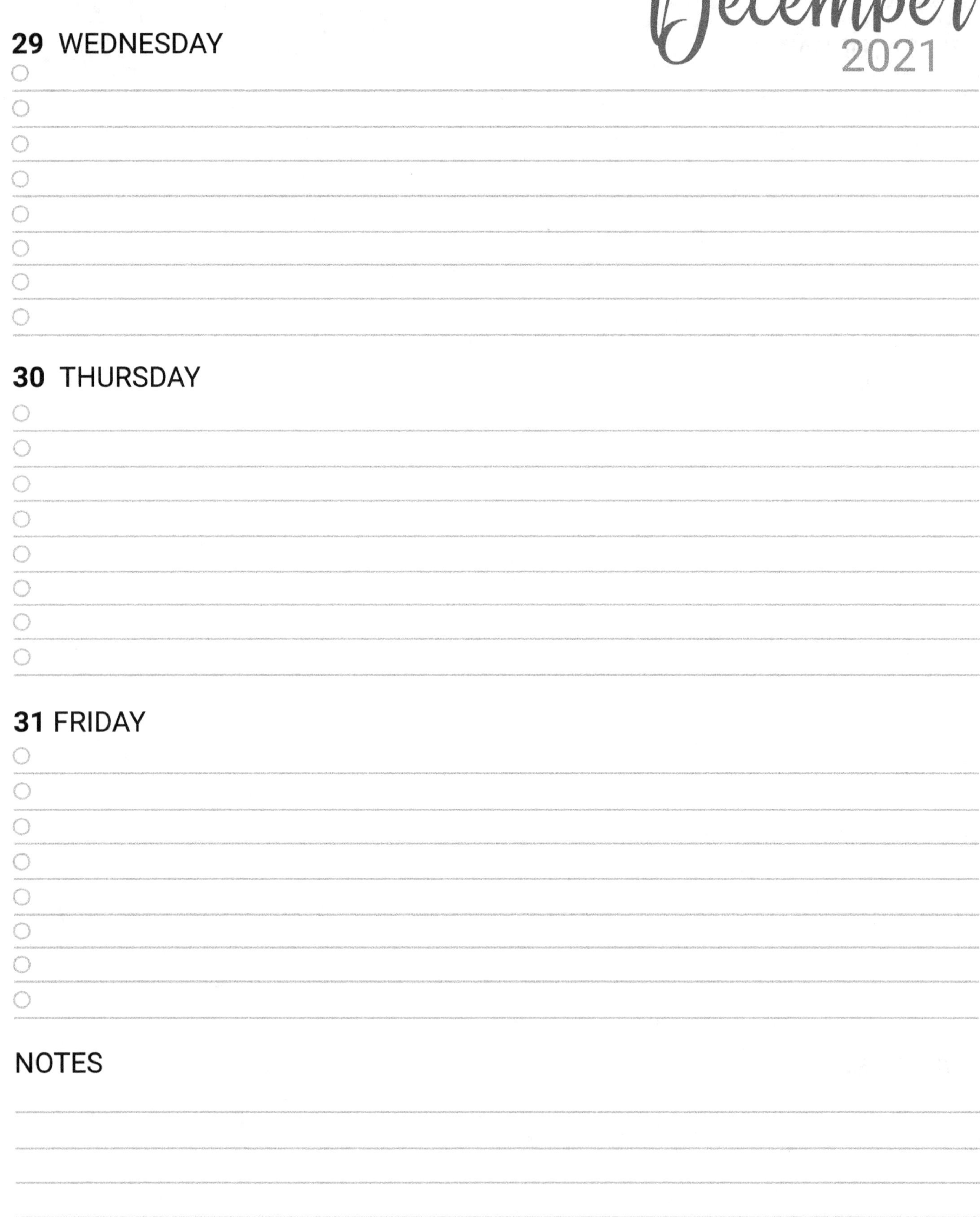



**29** WEDNESDAY

**30** THURSDAY

**31** FRIDAY

NOTES

www.ingramcontent.com/pod-product-compliance
Lightning Source LLC
Chambersburg PA
CBHW080451030726
47592CB00011B/3073